I Want To Know Christ: A Forty Day Journey To The Cross
Paul W. Arndt - 1st ed.

ISBN 0-9727903-0-6
FAITHWORKS® Publishing

Manufactured in the United States of America

FIRST PRINTING

I Want To Know Christ

a forty day journey to the cross

paul arndt

For My Family

Faye, Joshua, and Jacob
Besides Christ, you know me the best; like Christ,
you love me when I'm at my worst; and in between
the knowing and the loving, you're always there,
ready to forgive.

Mom and Dad
Thanks for dreaming, believing, and praying God's
"immeasurably more" for your son.

Connie and Richard
Thanks for giving me God's "immeasurably more"
wrapped up in the gift of your daughter.

**The Ministry Leadership Team, the Staff, and
Members of Faith Lutheran Church**
As I wrote these words, I thought of you.

* * *

*"When I came to you, brothers, I did not come
with eloquence or superior wisdom as I proclaimed to
you the testimony about God. For I resolved to
know nothing while I was with you except Jesus Christ
and him crucified.*

*I came to you in weakness and fear, and with much
trembling. My message and my preaching were not with
wise and persuasive words, but with a demonstration of
the Spirit's power, so that your faith might not rest on
men's wisdom, but on God's power."*

1 Corinthians 2:1-5

Acknowledgements

To the Discipleship Team at Faith Lutheran Church
You sparked the dream; you kindled the process; your
lives flame with a passion to know Christ.

To Mike Imirie
You took my muddling with the king's English and
made it worthy of the King.

To Sheila Emerson
You handled all of the details. Without you, there'd be a
manuscript but there wouldn't be any book.

To Mari Green
You captured in one image
what I tried to say in 40,000 words.

To Daniel Nagy
You made the cover, the text, and the words attractive
to the eye and appealing to the heart.

To All of Those Who Read the Manuscript
You mixed your honesty with a spoonful of honey.
I pray your words only made mine sweeter.

To Max Lucado

Ten years ago my dad gave me a copy of
God Came Near. As I read it, the miraculous happened;
the Word wrapped himself up in your words.

Through letters arranged on a page, God had come
near. After that, I knew *what* I wanted to do.
I wanted to write.

You taught me the power of words.

To Ken Gire

On my thirty-first birthday, my mom gave me
a copy of *Intense Moments With the Savior.*
I read it. I read it again, and again.
Then I read the rest of the *Moment's* series.

I wanted to write, but—like an apprentice—I had
plenty of passion with no skills. No tools.
You gave me my first toolbox.
You filled it with your own tools.
You let an apprentice look over your shoulder
and learn as you wrote.

You taught me the beauty of words.

Contents

Prologue

"I want to know Christ and the power of his resurrection and the fellowship of sharing in his sufferings, becoming like him in his death, and so, somehow, to attain to the resurrection from the dead."

Philippians 3:10-11

"I want to know Christ!"

That's a passionate prayer. Five sincere, short, one-syllable words that even a child could say. Though it's a simple prayer, the answer is complex. The process is surprising—even shocking—at times. Knowing Christ is a spiritual adventure that's full of uncharted territory, assorted terrain, and unknown destinations. It takes us on a long journey and it happens in a multitude of mysterious ways.

In this book, you'll find a set of navigational tools to help guide you on your way. Each day begins with a selected portion from one of the Gospels. Read the text from your own Bible and then reread it, asking the question, "What does this tell me about Christ?"

Following each reading is a prayer. Use the prayer to focus, direct, and capture the desire of your heart on that day. Apply it to your situation in life. Let it guide and shape your understanding of who Christ is. Come back to it throughout the day and allow it to do whatever work Christ may choose.

After the prayer is a brief, written meditation centered on the Scripture for the day. Read the meditation with a receptive heart, asking Christ to reveal himself through the words. The words aren't perfect. Neither are the thoughts behind them. Together, though, they just might be a means by which Christ may choose to speak.

Finally, there is a section for reflection. As with anything that requires work, the reward is in direct proportion to the effort. What you get out of this section is only a reflection of what you're willing to put in. Invest yourselves in the questions. Think deeply about them. Take time to ponder the meaning behind the moments of your life.

Scattered throughout the forty days are seven "Sabbaths". The first allows you to sit and rest awhile. The second provides you with a moment to remember the goodness and the grace of Christ in your life. The third stills the soul and prepares it for repentance. The fourth quiets your world and allows you to listen and respond to his voice. The fifth is a refreshing moment, a time to sit by the still waters and reflect on the journey thus far. The sixth gives a brief respite that relaxes the hands to receive whatever Christ would give. And finally, the seventh Sabbath is a day to rejoice in the new life of the resurrection.

My advice? During each "Sabbath" ...

Stop for a few moments.
　　Sit still.
　　　　Soak it all up.

It's my prayer that, after taking this forty-day journey, you might "know Christ". But, before we begin, let's be clear about the destination. What does it mean "to know Christ"? Here's an apprentice's answer to a journeyman's question:

To know Christ means ...

There's an intellectual understanding.
I know something *about* him.

There's an internal transformation.
I become more and more *like* him.

There's an intimate relationship.
I suffer, die, and rise *with* him.

During these forty days, may you learn more about Christ, may you become more and more like him, and may you share with him, not only in his sufferings, but also in his resurrection. Together, let's desire to know Christ. And along the way, may each one of us discover that he already knows us!

paul

Before You Begin

Why are you starting this spiritual journey? What are you looking for? What are you hoping to find?

In your wildest dreams, what do you think could happen during these forty days?

In what way do you want "to know Christ"?

Before you begin, write a prayer describing your desire for these forty days.

Day One:
The Tempted Christ

Scripture Reading: Matthew 3:13–4:11

Prayer

Father,

For forty days your Son wandered in the wilderness. In the barrenness, he fasted. In the darkness, he prayed. In the forsaken wasteland, he walked alone. And when he was at his weakest, he was tempted by the devil. Three times his enemy enticed him:

"Take care of yourself."
"Prove yourself."
"Indulge yourself."

Three times he was seduced. Three times he said, "No!" His response to each temptation was firm; his resolve didn't waver, and his resistance defined the means and manner of his Messianic ministry. He was the Son of Man, tempted in every way, just like us. He was also the Son of God—pure, holy, and without sin.

During this day, help me know the *Tempted Christ*. When the Tempter comes into my wilderness remind me that I have a Savior who knows what it's like to be tempted—tempted in every way—just like me. Comfort me with the fact that he is aware of my weaknesses. Remind me that he sympathizes with them. Assure me that, when I am tempted, he has promised that he will provide a way out. It's in his name that I pray. Amen

Meditation

Jesus begins his ministry by standing in a river. John the Baptist baptizes him. Heaven opens. The Spirit descends like a dove and the Father speaks. But while he is still wet, the Spirit leads him out into the desert. Immediately, he moves from the baptismal water to the barren wilderness, from the affirmation of the Father to the temptation of the evil one.

In the river, Jesus had heard his Father say from heaven, "This is my Son, whom I love; with him I am well pleased."[1] But now, in the wilderness, the Tempter counters his Father's words. Three times the evil one challenges the divine roots of his family tree, "If you are the Son of God ...".

So begins his ministry.

Before he calls any of the disciples, before he teaches or preaches, before he heals or performs one miracle, before he goes to the cross, comes out of the tomb, or ascends into heaven, before any and all of this, he spends forty days in the wilderness. During that time, he is tempted to quit his Messianic ministry before it even begins.

The wilderness is a time for prayer, fasting, and feasting on his Father's Word. After forty days of fasting, he's more than hungry. He's tired. He's weak. In a word, he's vulnerable. And that's when the Tempter comes.

In the hunger he entices,

> *"If you are the Son of God, tell these stones to become bread."* [2]

From the highest point of the temple he challenges,

> *"If you are the Son of God throw yourself down."* [3]

And into the barrenness, simplicity, and meekness of his life he scoffs, spreads his arms across the nations, and promises,

> *"All this I will give you if you will bow down and worship me."* [4]

With each temptation there's a price tag. But Jesus isn't buying. He has other things to spend his life on.

When tempted, Jesus doesn't delay or deliberate. He acts and speaks decisively. Three times he responds, "It is written ...". He doesn't rely on his own physical strength. Instead, in his weakness, he draws the sword of the Spirit. It's not a large sword; it's more like a dagger. It's short, sharp, and capable of swift stabs. He doesn't draw chapters of Scripture out of his sheath, but verses. Three times he jabs.

> *"Man does not live on bread alone, but on every word that comes from the mouth of God."* [5]

> *"Do not put the Lord your God to the test."* [6]

> *"Worship the Lord your God and serve him only."* [7]

"With a final lunge Jesus says, "Away from me, Satan!"[8] As the devil scurries, angels sprint to attend to him. But the Tempter only leaves knowing that there will be another place and another "opportune time".[9] There will be another wilderness, another place of forsakenness, and another vulnerable moment where Jesus will be tempted to save himself and challenged to prove himself to be the Son of God.

> *"In the same way the chief priests, the teachers of the law and the elders mocked him. 'He saved others,' they said, 'but he can't save himself! He's the King of Israel! Let him come down now from the cross, and we will believe in him. He trusts in God. Let God rescue him now if he wants him, for he said, 'I am the Son of God.' " In the same way the robbers who were crucified with him also heaped insults on him." [10]*

The cross is the Tempter's "opportune time". But this time, he doesn't speak directly to Jesus, as he did in the wilderness. At the cross his voice is disguised and dispersed throughout the crowd. He scoffs at Jesus through the chief priests. He taunts him through the teachers of the law. He mocks him through the elders and he even ridicules him through the two thieves that are crucified next to him. He tempts Jesus to save himself. As in the wilderness, he challenges him to prove his divinity.

But when Jesus is tempted, he holds fast to the cross. When challenged, he grips the sin of the world. When he's given the opportunity to choose between saving his own life and redeeming the life of his world, he chooses to buy back the world. From the river, through the wilderness, to the cross, Jesus serves his Father. When he dies, the Tempter leaves defeated, the angels attend, and the Father is worshiped.

> *"Jesus said to him, 'Away from me, Satan! For it is written: 'Worship the Lord your God, and serve him only.' "*

> *"Then the devil left him, and angels came and attended him." [11]*

[1]Matthew 3:17 [2]Matthew 4:3 [3]Matthew 4:6 [4]Matthew 4:9 [5]Deuteronomy 8:3 [6]Deuteronomy 6:16 [7]Deuteronomy 6:13 [8]Matthew 4:10 [9]Luke 4:13 [10]Matthew 27:41-44 [11]Matthew 4:10-11

Reflection

What is your wilderness? When are you the most
vulnerable to the tempter's attack?

What does the tempter whisper in your ear?

What portions of God's Word could you use to counter these temptations?

In what areas of your life would you like to hear the *Tempted Christ* speak, "Away, Satan!"?

Day Two:
The Calling Christ

Scripture Reading: Matthew 4:12-22

Prayer

Father,

As your Son began his ministry, he called common, ordinary men to follow him. He invited them, "Come." He directed them, "Follow me." And then he promised to transform them, "I will make you fishers of men." He asked them to leave their well-established lives. He challenged them to let go of their world and enter his. In a word, he asked them to become disciples—followers of Christ. And they did.

Holy Spirit, on this day, may I come to know the *Calling Christ*. Show me once again that it is not I who chose Christ but that it is Christ who chose me.

Remind me of the day when he walked into the middle of my ordinary life, the day when he said, "Come, follow me", and the moment that he promised that he would make me into something extraordinary for his kingdom.

During this day, whenever the *Calling Christ* says, "come", may I immediately leave "the nets" of my life behind and follow after him. It's in his name that I pray. Amen.

Meditation

After the temptation in the wilderness, Jesus leaves his home in Nazareth. He goes to the region of Galilee, and makes his home in the city of Capernaum.

> *"Leaving Nazareth, he went and lived in*
> *Capernaum, which was by the lake in the area of*
> *Zebulun and Naphtali—to fulfill what was said*
> *through the prophet Isaiah:*
>
> > *'Land of Zebulun and land of Naphtali, the way to*
> > *the sea, along the Jordan,*
> > *Galilee of the Gentiles—*
> > *the people living in darkness*
> > *have seen a great light;*
> > *on those living in the land of the*
> > *shadow of death*
> > *a light has dawned.' "* [1]

This is a prophetic relocation. Centuries earlier, the prophet Isaiah had foretold that, in Galilee of the Gentiles, the people who had lived in darkness would see a great light. In Jesus, the light of the world has just moved into the neighborhood.

After he settles in, he introduces himself to his neighbors, gets to know the area, and walks the streets, the hills and the seashore of the seaside village. Then, when he's ready, he begins to let his light shine. For those who live in the land of the shadow of death, his message is like the rising of the sun,

> *"Repent, for the kingdom of heaven is near."* [2]

Early one morning, as Jesus walks the seashore, he begins to think about the calling that the Father has given him:

"Leave heaven! Humble and make yourself nothing! Take the very nature of a servant. Be obedient to death—even, death on a cross. Let go of your world and go into mine. Preach and teach and heal. Suffer, die, and rise again on the third day. And then when that work is complete, send. Send men and women into the world as I have sent you." 3

But before he can send, he must call.

As Jesus looks down the seashore, he sees two brothers: Simon called Peter, and his brother Andrew. The brothers also live in Capernaum. They're not strangers. They're his neighbors. Every day they've seen Jesus. They've heard him speak. They've talked to him and about him. But today is not every day. Today these ordinary men are about to get an extraordinary calling.

"As Jesus was walking beside the Sea of Galilee, he saw two brothers, Simon called Peter and his brother Andrew. They were casting a net into the lake, for they were fishermen. 'Come, follow me,' Jesus said, 'and I will make you fishers of men.' At once they left their nets and followed him." 4

He invites them—"come". He directs them—"follow after me". He promises to transform them—"I will make you fishers of men." He asks them to leave their lives behind and follow him. And as soon as he asks, they begin to follow. They leave it all behind. Nets. Boats. Family. They become his disciples.

With Simon and Andrew following, Jesus continues to walk down the shore. He sees another set of brothers, James, son of Zebedee, and his brother, John. They, too, are fishermen. Jesus calls them and they immediately jump out of the boat they have been working in. They leave their father with the nets, wave a running goodbye, and follow Jesus. Where there was once one, now there are five. Soon there will be twelve and after that multitudes.

Jesus chooses these men to be his disciples. But he doesn't search them out because they have any extraordinary skills, talents, or abilities. They're fishermen. He doesn't ask them to follow him because they stand out in society. They're normal, ordinary, and unschooled men. He doesn't call them because of what they can do for him. He calls them because of what he can do for them.

He simply asks them to come and *be with him.* And because they are with him, he promises to do something extraordinary for, through, and in them. And when the world looks at these men, the only thing it will take note of is that they had been with him.

> *"When they saw the courage of Peter and John and realized that they were unschooled, ordinary men, they were astonished and they took note that these men had been with Jesus."* [5]

[1]Matthew 4:13-16 [2]Matthew 4:17 [3]Philippians 2:5-8 [4]Matthew 4:18-20 [5]Acts 4:13

Reflection

In what way is the *Calling Christ* saying to you, "Come"?

Where is he asking you to follow?

In order to follow the *Calling Christ*, what must you leave behind?

How will people know that you have been with Jesus?

Day Three:
The Healing Christ

Scripture Reading: Matthew 4:23-25

Prayer

Father,

As your Son began his ministry, news about him spread. He taught with authority, preached with power, and healed every disease and sickness.

Those who had nowhere else to go came to him. Those who had nothing else to try hurried to him. Those who had no one left to see were carried to him. Into their darkness he shined the light of truth. Into their desperation he proclaimed "good news". And into their despair he brought hope. He was the *Healing Christ*.

On this day, may I know the *Healing Christ* and may I be assured that the *Healing Christ* knows me. Remind me that he knows every disease, sickness, and source of pain in my life. Into my suffering may he give hope. Into the darkness of my despair may he proclaim his "good news". And into my heart of many questions may he reveal truth.

I pray this because ...

> I have nowhere else to go.
> I have no one else to see.
> I have nothing else to try.

It's in his healing name I pray. Amen.

Meditation

Regular, ordinary, everyday news doesn't make it to the front page. That space is reserved for the tragedies and the triumphs of life. The only news that spreads fast is good news or bad news. As Jesus begins his ministry, he's big news.

> *"Jesus went throughout Galilee, teaching in their synagogues, preaching the good news of the kingdom, and healing every disease and sickness among the people. News about him spread all over Syria, and people brought to him all who were ill with various diseases, those suffering severe pain, the demon-possessed, those having seizures, and the paralyzed, and he healed them."* [1]

Jesus begins his ministry with a display of power. He's teaching in the synagogues with authority. He's preaching the "good news of the kingdom" with conviction. And, he's healing every disease and sickness among the people! This type of news spreads.

It spreads throughout Syria and Galilee, the Decapolis (the Ten Cities), Jerusalem, Judea, and the region across the Jordan. And as it spreads, people come. And when they come, they don't come alone. They bring with them the sick, the suffering, those in pain, the distressed and the demon possessed. They come, not to listen to the *Teaching Christ*, or to hear the *Preaching Christ*; they come to be touched by the *Healing Christ*.

Those who come have nowhere else to go. They have seen every doctor. They have taken every pill. They have tried every therapy.

"No. I'm sorry, I've done all that I can."
"No. There is no one else that you can see."
"No. I'm sorry, there are no more options."

They have even prayed every prayer. But now there is new news—news of someone who might be able to help. There is news of someone who could help even when everyone else had said, "no".

The big news is that Jesus is saying, "yes". "Yes" to those in severe pain. "Yes" to the demon possessed. "Yes" to those whose bodies shake uncontrollably and "yes" to those whose bodies won't move at all. People from all over hear the stories, they see the lives that have been changed, and so they come. They bring their friends. Jesus heals every one of them, and then every one of them begins to follow him.

He cares and so he heals. But he also heals to declare to the world that he is the long awaited Messiah. The healings make the headlines but, more than that, they are part of prophetic fulfillment. Jesus is the one—the Messiah—that Isaiah had spoken about.

> *"When Jesus came into Peter's house, he saw Peter's mother-in-law lying in bed with a fever. He touched her hand and the fever left her, and she got up and began to wait on him.*
>
> *When evening came, many who were demon-possessed were brought to him, and he drove out the spirits with a word and healed all the sick. This was to fulfill what was spoken through the prophet Isaiah:*
>
> > *'He took up our infirmities and carried our diseases.' "* [2]

When Jesus heals he draws a crowd. But he wants to do more than that. He wants to build a spiritual community. Into this new community, he wants to proclaim the "good news of the kingdom of heaven" as well as explain the truths of the Scriptures.

The healing that he wants to give is much more than physical. It's emotional, intellectual, and—above all—it's spiritual. He hasn't come just to heal physical bodies. Why would he stop there? Why just the body? Why not the mind? Why not the soul?

On this day, the healing touch of his hand is in Galilee. He has healed every disease and sickness in that region. But one day he will make his way to Jerusalem. There he will suffer, die, and rise again on the third day. And from the cross he will give the ultimate healing to all of humanity—the forgiveness of sins and life eternal.

"Surely he took up our infirmities
and carried our sorrows,
yet we considered him stricken by God,
smitten by him, and afflicted.
But he was pierced for our transgressions,
he was crushed for our iniquities;
the punishment that brought us
peace was upon him,
and by his wounds we are healed." [3]

[1]Matthew 4:23-24 [2]Matthew 8:14-17 [3]Isaiah 53:4-5

Reflection

What type of healing could you ask the *Healing Christ* for?

Physical Healing:

Emotional Healing:

Intellectual Healing:

Spiritual Healing:

Day Four:
The Blessing Christ

Scripture Reading: Matthew 5:1-12

Prayer

Father,

As your Son began his ministry, large crowds followed him. Seeing the multitudes, he went up on a mountainside, sat down, and began to teach. His disciples sat around him and he explained to them what life in the kingdom of God was like. He said that, in him, they would be blessed. He assured them that they would have more than the world could offer. He promised them that they would have nothing less than God's best.

But he also warned them. He told them that they would be insulted, persecuted, and all kinds of false things would be said about them. Because of him, they would be exposed to the world's worst.

As he taught, he proclaimed the "blessed" paradox of life in the kingdom of heaven. Through eight beatitudes, he promised God's best in the midst of the world's worst.

During this day, help me experience the blessedness that comes with Christ. As I wait for God's best in the midst of the world's worst, may I desire something more than pleasure. May I long for something more than joy. May I yearn for something more than happiness. As I wait, may I crave nothing more and nothing less than the presence of Christ. It's in his name I pray. Amen.

Meditation

As Jesus heals every disease and sickness among the people of Galilee, news spreads, and large crowds begin to follow him. Not far from Capernaum, at the northwest corner of the Sea of Galilee, there's a gently sloping hillside. Jesus climbs the hill, comes to a plateau, and sits down. His disciples come to him and he begins to teach them about life in the kingdom of God. He begins with eight declarations of "blessedness". Eight beatitudes.

The disciples who sit at his feet have left everything to follow him. They have forsaken family, occupation, and worldly security. They sit at his feet and eagerly await his first words about the kingdom of God. They know what they have given up, but they don't know what they're going to get in return.

His words aren't what they expect. They don't promise power, privilege, or prestige. They're words of poverty, grief, humility, and hunger. He speaks of charity, purity and peace—character traits and conditions not often found in their world. And he warns of persecution—persecution that hurts on earth but that brings a great reward in heaven. He begins each statement about the kingdom with the word "blessed".

It's a relational word. There's always someone *behind*, or *in*, or *with* the blessing:

"God bless you."
"Blessings in what you do."
"Go with God's blessing."

Eight times Jesus says, "blessed". Eight times he connects it to someone who needs blessing. Eight times he speaks his best into the world's worst. When Jesus says, "blessed", he is assuring his disciples that in the midst of the world's worst he will be present. He'll give them nothing less than his best.

"Blessed" is also a kingdom word. Jesus takes a word that they know and he gives it a new definition. He redefines the word and—in the process—redefines their world.

If they are to follow Jesus they must learn that "blessed", in his kingdom, has nothing to do with political power or socioeconomic strata. It doesn't deal with heads of state, or gold, or silver; rather, its concern and its currency is that of the cross—commodities such as grace, mercy and peace. These are the riches of Christ and the foundation of life in the kingdom of God.

When the world is at its worst, Jesus gives nothing less than his best. He gives himself.

Blessed are ...

The poor in spirit.

The *Blessing Christ* pays the debt for the spiritually bankrupt.

Those who mourn.

The *Blessing Christ* embraces the lonely.

The meek.

The *Blessing Christ* uses the humble in heavenly ways.

Those who hunger and thirst for righteousness.

> The *Blessing Christ* satisfies those who search for God.

The merciful.

> The *Blessing Christ* reaches a hand down to those who have a hand up.

The pure in heart.

> To those who want to see God, the *Blessing Christ* makes them clean from the inside out.

The peacemakers.

> When things go wrong the *Blessing Christ* makes things right.

Those who are persecuted.

> The *Blessing Christ* gives eternal pleasures to those who are picked on, punched out, and put down on account of his name.

Reflection

In what area of your life do you need Christ to say, "blessed"?

What beatitude are you living in right now?

How have you been persecuted for being a follower of Christ? What do you think the eternal reward for such persecutions will be?

Why is "blessedness" something more than pleasure, joy, or happiness? Why does it only exist in the person and presence of Christ?

Sabbath Day of Rest

*"Come to me, all you who are weary and burdened,
and I will give you rest. Take my yoke upon you and learn
from me, for I am gentle and humble in heart, and you
will find rest for your souls. For my yoke is easy and
my burden is light."*

Matthew 11:28-30

Rest. It's a precious gift and yet it's so rarely opened.
Busyness and business have pushed the gift off to the
side. In order to open the gift, one has to slow down, sit
still, turn down the volume, and give up control.

See this Sabbath rest as a divine exchange. On this day,
Christ desires to take something away from you as well
as give you something in return. He wants to exchange
weariness for his open arms, turmoil for his tranquility,
and burdens for his blessing.

Reflection

During the first four days of your journey, how has Christ given you rest?

How is Christ asking you to slow down, sit still, and give up control?

What divine exchange does Christ want to work in you?

Day Five:
The Sending Christ

Scripture Reading: Matthew 9:35-10:42

Prayer

Father,

As your Son looked upon the crowds, he had compassion. He saw them as sheep without a shepherd—harassed, helpless, and vulnerable to attack. There were so many who were hurting and so few ready and able to help. And so he asked his disciples to pray. He said,

> *"Ask the Lord of the harvest to send out workers into his harvest field."* [1]

They asked and then they became the answer. The *Sending Christ* commissioned them. He gave them his authority. He directed them where to go. He told them what to say. He explained to them what to do. And, as they left, he warned them. He comforted them. He promised them that he would walk the harvest fields with them.

During this day, I ask that the *Sending Christ* show me where my world is ready, waiting, and ripe for a kingdom harvest. Send me to those who are harassed and helpless. Lead me to those who are lost and looking for the Good Shepherd. Impassion me. Commission me. Empower me. And as I go, make my feet swift, strong, and beautiful. It's in the *Sending Christ's* name that I pray and it's in his power that I go. Amen

Meditation

Before any great commission is given, there must be great compassion. First the heart has to be moved, and then the feet. The Sending Christ does both. He moves the heart of his disciples and then he moves their feet.

"When he saw the crowds, he had compassion on them, because they were harassed and helpless, like sheep without a shepherd. Then he said to his disciples, 'The harvest is plentiful but the workers are few. Ask the Lord of the harvest, therefore, to send out workers into his harvest field.' " [2]

As Jesus looks on the crowd, his heart breaks. He sees so many needs and yet there are so few hands to help. He senses so much pain and yet there are so few arms to comfort. He's aware of so many people who are ready to hear the good news of the kingdom of God yet there are so few mouths ready to speak. He compares the crowd to a flock of sheep. They have no shepherd. They're harassed, helpless, vulnerable, lost, and open to attack.

His compassion compels him to act. He prays. He looks for the answer and finds it in twelve men. He calls his disciples and commissions them.

These twelve are the dirty dozen. Simon Peter and John are "unschooled, ordinary men"[3]. Matthew works for the Roman internal revenue service. The other Simon is a zealot. Thomas will question the resurrection and will never shake the moniker of "doubter". And Judas Iscariot, his name will be synonymous with "traitor".

The twelve disciples aren't well polished. They aren't even diamonds in the rough. They're just rough. But the harvest is plentiful and the workers are few, so a dozen rough men are better than no men at all.

As he calls them he gives them a gem of a message.

"The kingdom of heaven is near." 4

He empowers them.

"Heal the sick, raise the dead, cleanse those who have leprosy, drive out demons. Freely you have received, freely give." 5

He instructs them.

"Go here. Don't go there. Do this. Bring that. Look for opportunities and watch out for enemies."

He assures them of his presence.

"He who receives you receives me, and he who receives me receives the one who sent me." 6

This isn't just a mission; this is a co-mission. The *Sending Christ* is going with them and—as he goes with them—he promises that he will give them the right words to say at the right time.

"But when they arrest you, do not worry about what to say or how to say it. At that time you will be given what to say, for it will not be you speaking, but the Spirit of your Father speaking through you." 7

The Messiah, who carries the most important message that the world would ever hear, decides to place that divine message into messy human hands. He takes his words and places them into his disciple's mouths. He doesn't declare his message through a booming voice. He speaks through the stutters of common men.

God has a Galilean accent.

This is how he reaps his harvest—word-by-word, conversation-by-conversation, life-by-life. As his disciples listen, he listens. When they speak, he speaks. When they act, he acts. It's a co-mission. They walk the harvest fields together.

> *"How, then, can they call on the one they have not believed in? And how can they believe in the one of whom they have not heard? And how can they hear without someone preaching to them? And how can they preach unless they are sent? As it is written, 'How beautiful are the feet of those who bring good news!' "* [8]

[1]Matthew 9:38 [2]Matthew 9:36-38 [3]Acts 4:13 [4]Matthew 10:7 [5]Matthew 10:8 [6]Matthew 10:40 [7]Matthew 10:19-20 [8]Romans 10:14-15

Reflection

What is your harvest field?

Who in your life is ready and waiting to hear the good news?

The *Sending Christ* promises that the Holy Spirit will give you the right words at the right time. How does that encourage you to speak the good news?

What comfort does it bring you to know that the *Sending Christ* walks with you through the harvest field?

Day Six:
The Teaching Christ

Scripture Reading: Matthew 13:1-58

Prayer

Father,

When your Son taught, he used parables. He took the common, simple, ordinary things of our earthly life—a sower sowing seed, weeds, yeast, a mustard seed, a hidden treasure, and a net—and used them to describe the height and depth of his eternal kingdom. He told stories and thereby illustrated what life in the kingdom of heaven was like. He made divine mysteries manageable for the human mind.

As he taught, he spoke our language. He started with something that we knew and, from there, taught us something that we didn't know. He took the things that we've always seen, always been around, always known, and connected it to something that we had never seen, never been around, never known. He collided his heavenly mysteries with the mundane moments of our lives. The result of that collision was revelation. Our eyes were opened and we saw what the kingdom of heaven was really like.

On this day, I ask that the *Teaching Christ* reveal to me the truth about the kingdom of heaven. When I hear but don't understand, when I see but don't perceive, or when my heart is calloused and cold, may he enter my world, use the things around me, speak my language, and say to me in an intimate way, "The kingdom of heaven is like ...". And when he speaks, may I have ears to hear. In his name I pray. Amen.

Meditation

The crowds have forced Jesus off the shore and into a boat. As he sits down in the boat, he begins to teach many things about the kingdom of heaven. But as he teaches, he speaks to the crowd in parables—gritty, illustrative, simple stories that take the mysteries of God and demystify them. His parables make divine mysteries manageable for the human mind.

"That same day Jesus went out of the house and sat by the lake. Such large crowds gathered around him that he got into a boat and sat in it, while all the people stood on the shore. Then he told them many things in parables, saying: 'A farmer went out to sow his seed.'" [1]

After his first parable, Jesus says to the crowd,

"He who has ears to hear let him hear." [2]

Tragically, many in the crowd have come to listen but not many have come to learn. Their hearts are calloused and closed to the truth; they hear his words, but they don't understand what he is trying to say. They see him with their own eyes but they don't perceive who he really is. The Truth is in their midst, but only a few recognize and receive it. The prophet Isaiah foretold all of this.

"In them is fulfilled the prophecy of Isaiah:

   'You will be ever hearing but never
     understanding;
   you will be ever seeing but never
     perceiving.
   For this people's heart has become
     calloused;
   they hardly hear with their ears,

and they have closed their eyes.
Otherwise they might see with their eyes,
hear with their ears,
understand with their hearts
and turn, and I would heal them.' " 3

To those who have ears to hear, the *Teaching Christ* tells seven parables. He takes familiar things—a sower sowing seed, weeds, a mustard seed, yeast, a hidden treasure, a pearl and a net—and infuses those earthy vessels with something far beyond human understanding. He fills the stories with the truths of the kingdom of heaven.

"The kingdom of heaven is like a man who sowed good seed in his field." 4

"The kingdom of heaven is like a mustard seed, which a man took and planted in his field." 5

"The kingdom of heaven is like treasure hidden in a field." 6

"Again, the kingdom of heaven is like a merchant looking for fine pearls." 7

"Once again, the kingdom of heaven is like a net that was let down into the lake and caught all kinds of fish." 8

Jesus teaches. He reveals. He speaks his disciples' language. He shows them something higher and deeper, above and beyond, something surpassing their dreams, imaginations, and understanding. He shows them the secrets of the kingdom of heaven. Even more incredible, through the parables Jesus reveals himself.

He's the sower who sows the good seed.

He's the treasure in the field.

He's the pearl of great price.

He's the point of the parables.

He's the kingdom of heaven in their midst.

He's the Message and he's the Messenger.

He's the Way and he makes the way.

He is Life and he gives life.

As Jesus teaches, his disciples are learning from him, but more importantly they are learning about him.

He who has ears to hear let him hear.

[1]Matthew 13:1-3 [2]Matthew 13:9 [3]Matthew 13:14-15 [4]Matthew 13:24
[5]Matthew 13:31 [6]Matthew 13:44 [7]Matthew 13:45 [8]Matthew 13:47

Reflection

What does the *Teaching Christ* mean when he says, "he who has ears to hear let him hear"?

What do you need to learn from the *Teaching Christ?* What do you need to learn about him?

How has the *Teaching Christ* used the ordinary things around you to illustrate the kingdom of God?

What type of parables is Christ speaking in your life? How is Jesus revealing himself to you?

Day Seven:
The Transfigured Christ

Scripture Reading: Matthew 16:13–17:13

Prayer

Father,

During your Son's earthly ministry, he didn't always use his divine power or fully reveal his divine nature. In his state of humiliation, he took on human flesh. He wrapped the veil of his humanity around his eternal majesty, and hid his glory.

But on the Mount of Transfiguration, he lifted the veil. His glory blazed, his face shone like the sun, his clothes became as white as snow, and his disciples became eyewitnesses of his majesty.

During this day, I want to see, through the veil of my humanity, glimpses of the *Transfigured Christ*. May his face shine in the darkness and despair of my life. May his presence blaze in my world. I want to be an eyewitness of his majesty. And when I see his majesty, may I be transformed into his likeness. In Jesus name I pray. Amen

Meditation

The ups and downs of Peter's emotions follow the contour of the mountain that he is now descending. Seven days ago, Jesus asked his disciples who they thought he was. They said that the people had all types of opinions: John the Baptist, Elijah, Jeremiah, or one of the prophets. Each opinion was wrong—all except Peter's.

> " *'But what about you?' he asked. 'Who do you say I am?'*
>
> *Simon Peter answered, 'You are the Christ, the Son of the living God.'*
>
> *Jesus replied, 'Blessed are you, Simon son of Jonah, for this was not revealed to you by man, but by my Father in heaven.' "* [1]

Peter was the only one who got it right.

It was the Father who had revealed to Peter that Jesus was the Messiah. After his confession, Peter was on the mountaintop. He understood who Jesus was, "the Christ, the Son of the living God." But as the events of the week progressed, it became clear that Peter didn't understand, nor did he like, what this Jesus was about to do. He might have understood the person of Christ but he didn't understand his work.

When Jesus spoke of his suffering, death, and resurrection, Peter rebuked him. To which Jesus turned to Peter and said,

> *"Get behind me, Satan!"* [2]

Within a span of minutes, Peter had moved from the mountain of revelation to the valley of rebuke. In the valley he's confused, unclear, and uncertain about what it means to follow Jesus. Though Peter has bottomed out, Jesus buoys him up.

> *"I tell you the truth, some who are standing here will not taste death before they see the Son of Man coming in his kingdom."* [3]

Six days later, Jesus invites Peter, James, and John to follow him up a mountain. It's time they get a glimpse of his majesty. On the mountaintop, he's transfigured. His appearance is altered from the inside out. He doesn't turn into someone else. He shows his disciples who he really is.

He lifts the veil of his humanity and lets the divinity blaze in all its glory. From the inside out, his face shines like the sun. His clothes become as white as light. Moses and Elijah appear and talk with him and a voice from a cloud shouts,

> *"This is my Son, whom I love; with him I am well pleased. Listen to him!"* [4]

The disciples are eyewitnesses to his majesty. They have just seen the Son of Man coming in his kingdom.

But being on the mountain is one thing; staying there is another. Jesus can't stay. He won't stay, even though the disciples offer to build three shelters—one for Moses, the Lawgiver; one for Elijah, the representative of the prophets; and one for Jesus, the Messiah, the fulfillment of all that went before. Though the disciples plead with him to stay, he insists that it's time to descend the mountain.

He must walk toward Jerusalem and then walk up another mountain—Calvary. While Moses and Elijah were with him on the Mount of Transfiguration, they talked with Jesus about his crucifixion.

"They spoke about his departure, which he was about to bring to fulfillment at Jerusalem." [5]

The Mount of Transfiguration.
The Mount of Crucifixion.

Both mountains give a glimpse of his glory. One blazes from the inside out. The other bleeds from the outside in.

On the Mount of Transfiguration, Jesus' divinity bursts through human flesh and shines like the sun. On this summit, he reveals his glory. He pulls back the veil that covers his majesty. Nothing is hidden. All is revealed. God is seen as God, and he is *among* his creation!

On the Mount of Crucifixion, the suffering of the Son of Man pierces the heart of the Father. On this summit, Jesus reveals his grace. His love blazes in the darkness of sin. His salvation shines. Forgiveness flares for all to see. At the cross, when humanity is showing God its worst, there Christ is, arms stretched out wide, showing humanity God's best. Again, nothing is hidden. All is revealed. All is given. He is God, but more than that, he is good. On this mountain, God is *for* his creation!

> *"We did not follow cleverly invented stories when we told you about the power and coming of our Lord Jesus Christ, but we were eyewitnesses of his majesty. For he received honor and glory from God the Father when the voice came to him from the Majestic Glory, saying, 'This is my Son, whom I love; with him I am well pleased.' We ourselves heard this voice that came from heaven when we were with him on the sacred mountain."* [6]

[1]Matthew 16:15-17 [2]Matthew 16:23 [3]Matthew 16:28 [4]Matthew 17:5
[5]Luke 9:30-31 [6]2 Peter 1:16-18

Reflection

If Jesus were to ask you, "who do you say that I am?", what would you say?

How has the *Transfigured Christ* shown you his glory?

How has the *Crucified Christ* shown you his glory?

What does your story about Christ consist of? In what way are you an "eyewitnesses of his majesty"?

Day Eight:
The Solitary Christ

Scripture Reading: Mark 1:21-39

Prayer

Father,

One morning, while it was still dark out, your Son got up, left the house and went off to a solitary place where he prayed. In that early hour, he didn't sneak away from the house in order to escape the crowds; he stole away in order to be with you. He didn't run away from the sick, the dying, and the demon possessed; he ran towards you. He left the house so that he might return renewed, refreshed, and rededicated to your purpose for his life.

On this day, may I—like the *Solitary Christ*—practice the spiritual discipline of *"leaving"*. During this day, may I get up and leave, if only for a few moments, the demands, responsibilities, business, and busyness of my life and go to a solitary place ...

> a place of silence,
> > of intimacy,
> > > of time spent solely with you.

After being with you, may I practice the spiritual discipline of *"returning"*. May I return with a divine determination to begin, continue, or finish the work you have given me. It's in your Son's name that I pray. Amen

Meditation

Jesus is a man who fits forty-eight hours worth of work in twenty-four hour days. He teaches. He casts out demons. He heals the sick. He's busy doing his Father's business. But Jesus knows that, when you work with people, there's always more to do. There's always one more lesson that could be taught, one more problem that could and should be solved, and one more person who would like to be healed.

> *"That evening after sunset the people brought*
> *to Jesus all the sick and demon-possessed. The*
> *whole town gathered at the door, and Jesus healed*
> *many who had various diseases. He also drove*
> *out many demons, but he would not let the*
> *demons speak because they knew who he was."* [1]

He's been busy doing but now it's time for him to spend some moments *being—being* alone, *being* quiet, *being* with his Father.

He gets up very early in the morning while it's still dark. He leaves the house in which he's been staying and goes off to a solitary place. He practices the discipline of *"leaving"*.

He leaves the crowds. He leaves the activity. He leaves the pace of his world and enters the place of solitude. This *"leaving"* isn't an escape; it's an embrace. He's not running away from his ministry. He's not running away from responsibilities. He's running to his Father. He's leaving the many to be with the One. He wants to hear one voice. He longs to know only one heart. His desire is to be one with the Father and so he looks for a solitary place.

When he finds that solitary place, he begins to pray. In the solitude, few words are spoken but much is said. He is refreshed by the message that comes through the silence. This place is quiet. It's intimate. It's special. It's one of the few times and rare places where he can just be and not have to do. Here he can be still and know his Father. Here his Father can know him.

But the solitude doesn't last.

> *"Simon and his companions went to look for him, and when they found him, they exclaimed: 'Everyone is looking for you!' "* [2]

As the sun rises, Simon notices that Jesus isn't in the house. He's not outside with Simon's mother-in-law. He's not with the crowds who had gathered at the door the night before. He's not by the seashore, either. No one's seen him since last night.

And so, Simon and his companions go looking for him. They walk the shore. They climb the hills. They shout his name. Finally, they find him, sitting alone, face toward the morning sun. They invade the solitude and break the silence by exclaiming,

> "Everyone is looking for you!"
> "What are you doing out here?"
> "The people need you!"

It's time to leave the solitary place. His face still warming in the sun, Jesus says,

> *" 'Let us go somewhere else—to the nearby villages—so I can preach there also. That is why I have come.' So he traveled throughout Galilee, preaching in their synagogues and driving out demons."* [3]

Without delay, disappointment, or resentment, Jesus gets up, walks away from the secret place and walks toward the public place. He abandons the discipline of *"leaving"* and embraces the discipline of *"returning."* He doesn't fight the call back to the busyness and the *doing* of his ministry. Rather, he delights in it. He returns to the people, the places, and the problems. He returns to the duties, demands, and expectations. When he returns, he's refreshed.

In the intimate moments, his Father had whispered his favor. He had anointed him with divine determination, placed his hand of blessing upon him, and given him peace. In the solitude, his Father had reminded him of his purpose.

"My Son, you *must* begin this journey to the cross."
"You *must* continue to teach, preach, and heal."
"You *must* finish the work that I have given you."

In the solitude, Jesus had heard his Father's voice. Having heard his voice, he's ready to leave. But as he leaves, the Father also gives him an invitation to return ...

My son, "be still, and know that I am God". [4]

[1]Mark 1:32-34 [2]Mark 1:36-37 [3]Mark 1:38-39 [4]Psalm 46:10

Reflection

In what way are you practicing the spiritual discipline of "leaving"? How are you "getting up, leaving the house, and finding a solitary place"?

How are you practicing the spiritual discipline of "returning"?

How does your time alone with the *Solitary Christ* impact your world?

What is the divine *must* that the Father reminds you of in the time of solitude?

Day Nine:
The Calming Christ

Scripture Reading: Mark 4:35-41

Prayer

Father,

Before the storm set upon the sea, your Son said to his disciples,

"Let us go over to the other side." [1]

Halfway across, a furious squall came up. Waves broke over the boat and it was in danger of being swamped. Even more troubling was the fact that, during all of this, your Son was asleep. His disciples shook him awake and asked,

"Teacher, don't you care if we drown?" [2]

They wondered if he knew what was happening. They questioned if he cared. They were uncertain if he would help. He did help. He got up and rebuked the wind and the waves. The sea became calm.

During this day, remind me that though the *Calming Christ* doesn't always prevent the storms from happening, he does promise to enter them. He is aware of them. He is present in them. He still says, "Quiet! Be still!" Help me believe that this *Calming Christ* cares about my life and that he is the same powerful God before, after, and during the storm. It's in his name that I pray. Amen

Meditation

It was Jesus' idea.

> *"That day when evening came, he said to his disciples, 'Let us go over to the other side.' Leaving the crowd behind, they took him along, just as he was, in the boat. There were also other boats with him."* [3]

Halfway across the sea, the disciples wonder if Jesus had made a mistake.

> *"A furious squall came up, and the waves broke over the boat, so that it was nearly swamped."* [4]

None of the disciples saw it coming. The cool air from the Mediterranean had slithered through the narrow mountain passes. When it got close to the water in the Galilean basin, it raised its head, shot upward, and blind-sided the hot, humid air hanging over the Sea of Galilee. This collision didn't create a storm; it sired a squall. It was an offspring that was rebellious, violent, and deadly.

Gale winds blew. They created whitecaps that dumped wave after wave into the boat. The disciples bailed furiously but, for every bucket they threw overboard, five buckets returned. They knew that if something didn't happen soon, if someone didn't help, if in some way this squall didn't stop, this could be *it*. This could be the way their lives end.

> *"Jesus was in the stern, sleeping on a cushion. The disciples woke him and said to him, 'Teacher, don't you care if we drown?' "* [5]

While the squall rages, Jesus sleeps. He's snoring in the stern of the boat. Exhausted. Even the spray of the waves, the thrashing of the boat, the flashes of lightning, and the blasts of thunder can't stir him. Divinity is sleeping in a human body. Snoring. He's dreaming in the middle of the disciples' nightmare. His disciples shake him. They shout above the thunder, "Teacher, don't you care if we drown? Wake up!"

They wonder if he is aware. They question if he cares. His actions answer their question.

> *"He got up, rebuked the wind and said to the waves, 'Quiet! Be still!' Then the wind died down and it was completely calm.*
>
> *He said to his disciples, 'Why are you so afraid? Do you still have no faith?'*
>
> *They were terrified and asked each other, 'Who is this? Even the wind and the waves obey him!' "* [6]

Jesus wakes up, stands firm in the stern, steadies himself, and speaks into the wind,

"Quiet! Be still!"

As suddenly as the squall came, it leaves. The wind dies down, the waves disappear, and it is completely calm. With three words, he silences the sea. Those three words show his disciples that he is aware of the fury of the squall and that he does care about their lives. They show that he is more than able and willing to act.

But when he calms the sea, the squall doesn't cease; it turns inward.

Moments before, when the disciples were in the middle of the storm, they shouted at Jesus. They had wondered if he was aware of the danger. They had accused him of not caring. After he spoke, silenced the waves, and stilled the sea—all for which they prayed—another storm begins: an inner storm.

A collision occurs between their humanity and his divinity. There is turbulence between their human reason and his divine revelation. The chilling winds of their doubt, fear, and unbelief collide with the warm winds of his faithfulness, power, and majesty.

He has shown them something that they weren't expecting to see. He has done something that they can't understand. He has just wrestled, grabbed, and tamed the wind. As a result, they're in turmoil. They're terrified. They wonder, "Who is this? Even the winds and the waves obey him!" It's a crisis of faith. Though the outer storm has ended, an inner storm begins.

Jesus, however, speaks into both storms.

> He speaks into the outer storm.
> > He silences the furious squalls of their life.
> > "Quiet!"

> He speaks into the inner storm.
> > He calms the chilling winds of their doubt.
> > "Be still!"

He doesn't prevent the storm from happening, but he does promise to enter it.

[1]Mark 4:35 [2]Mark 4:38 [3]Mark 4:35-36 [4]Mark 4:37 [5]Mark 4:38 [6]Mark 4:39-41

Reflection

Describe a time in your life when a "furious squall" suddenly came upon you?

In what ways have you shaken the *Sleeping Christ* and asked, "Don't you care if we drown?"

What types of storms are there in your life?
(Outer/Inner)

In what areas of your life do you need the *Calming Christ* to say, "Quiet! Be still!"?

The Miraculous Christ
Scripture Reading: Mark 4:35–5:43

Prayer

Father,

Through miracles, your Son revealed his divinity. He manifested his power and he demonstrated compassion. In the impossibilities of the helpless, the hopeless, and the hurting, he intervened.

He subdued the violent forces of nature. He vanquished a legion of demons. He loosened the grip of disease that had held a woman for twelve years. He conquered death. Through him, divine power invaded human problems and our impossibilities became his possibilities.

During this day, I want to know the person, the power, and the compassion of the *Miraculous Christ*. I want to know what he can do. I want to know what he will do. Above all, I want to know that he cares: cares enough to intervene in some miraculous way in my life. In this day, may the *Miraculous Christ* say to me,

"Don't be afraid; just believe."[1]

It's in his name that I pray. Amen

Meditation

Miracles. They display divinity. They manifest power. They demonstrate compassion. Over the course of a few days, Jesus stuns his world.

He tames the natural realm.

With three words, "Quiet! Be still!" the winds cease, the waves flatten, and the sea is stilled. [2]

He hogties and humiliates the supernatural realm.

He commands a legion of demons to come out of a man. For years they had possessed, imprisoned, and tormented him. But now they obey Jesus. They rush into a herd of pigs, which run down a steep bank, dive into the lake, and drown. [3]

He intervenes in the realm of life.

As he walks through a crowd, a woman sneaks up, reaches out and touches his garment. In return, his grace sneaks up, reaches in, and changes her life. "Go in peace and be freed from your suffering!" [4]

He loots the realm of death.

Jairus comes to Jesus more as a father than a synagogue ruler. Finding Jesus, he falls at his feet. He pleads with him to come and heal his twelve-year-old daughter. Jesus goes with him and, as Jairus walks with Jesus, he asks himself the question, "Can Jesus really heal my daughter?"

On their way, a sick woman in the crowd waylays Jesus. As he holds her hands, Jairus rings his. For twelve years she has suffered but now she is free. After she receives her miracle, they're back on their way. Jairus has his answer, "Jesus can heal. There's hope."

But as they approach Jairus' home the hope is taken away. It's too late. Jesus has taken too long. He has moved too slowly. The daughter has died.

Jairus' grief ignites a flurry of questions,

"Why didn't Jesus heal my daughter?"
"Why were we delayed?"
"Why were we too late?"

They're questions that rise up from a father's greatest fear—the loss of a child.

But in between the mysterious delay of the pleading for the miracle and the receiving of it, Jesus says to Jairus, "Don't be afraid; just believe." He goes to the little girl, takes her limp hand, and says, "Little girl, I say to you, get up!" Immediately, she gets up and he gives her back to her parents. 5

Life in a sinful world is filled with impossibilities. Nature rebels. The supernatural revolts. The body breaks down, the emotions break up, and relationships break off. It's a world full of grief, groans, and sighs. The danger that Jesus sees is that his world is getting used to it.

The crowds have embraced and accepted the status quo. Their lives have become mundane. They have elected not to expect the unexpected. They have chosen to believe that nothing in their life is going to, will, or can change.

"Life is the way it is, so don't get your hopes up."
"Don't challenge the way things are."
"Settle for something less instead of
hoping for God's 'immeasurably more'." 6

But Jesus doesn't come to maintain the status quo. He comes to challenge it. He wants to redeem and redefine it. He breaks the stupor of normality through miracles.

His miracles act as spiritual stimulants. They arouse attention. They excite, inspire, and inflame thoughts of what could be. They pique interest, prompt questions, and provoke emotions. They are God's possibilities invading human impossibilities. Miracles shatter normalcy. After a miracle, nothing and no one are the same.

The demon-possessed man isn't the same.
The woman in the crowd isn't the same.
Jairus and his family aren't the same.

The *Miraculous Christ* doesn't reveal the reason why he calms one storm and allows another to rage. He doesn't explain why he heals one, emotionally frees another, and relationally restores someone else, but doesn't do the same for others. He doesn't give a reason; he just gives a revelation.

He demonstrates that he cares.
He proves that he is in control.
He promises that he's close.

Maybe that's miracle enough.

1Mark 5:36 2Mark 4:35-41 3Mark 5:1-20 4Mark 5:24-34 5Mark 5:21-43
6Ephesians 3:20

Reflection

List the "impossibilities" of your life.

What miracle are you asking the *Miraculous Christ* for?

What miracles have you asked for in the past but didn't receive? What was your reaction? How did it affect your faith in the *Miraculous Christ*?

List the miracles that the *Miraculous Christ* has done in your life.

Sabbath Day of Remembrance

"Remember that you were slaves in Egypt and that the Lord your God brought you out of there with a mighty hand and an outstretched arm. Therefore the Lord your God has commanded you to observe the Sabbath day."

Deuteronomy 5:15

As we make our way into the forty-day journey, it's easy to forget where we were before it all started, what we were like before we took our first step, and why we began. This Sabbath Day provides you with a moment to stop and remember the goodness and the grace of Christ. Spend a few moments and look back over the last ten days.

Reflection

What were you like before the forty-day journey started? How were you "slaves in Egypt"?

How has Christ changed you during this journey? Are you becoming more and more like him?

What has Christ shown you about himself? Is the relationship growing more intimate? Are you sharing in his sufferings and the power of his resurrection?

Day Eleven:
The Compassionate Christ

Scripture Reading: Mark 6:30-44

Prayer

Father,

When your Son ministered to the needs of the many, he realized that there would always be too few hours in the day, too few hands to help, and too few resources to give. Those who came always asked him to do much with little. And when they kept coming, he looked on them with compassion.

He didn't see them as an inconvenience or an interruption or even an irritation. Rather, he was intimately aware of their needs. He cared deeply about their distress and he was willing to share and walk with them in their pain. In their suffering, he was a companion—a man of compassion.

During this day, I ask that the *Compassionate Christ* walk with me through the sufferings of my life. When I am used up, worn down, overwhelmed, and under stress, may he extend his hand and say to me,

"Come with me by yourselves to a quiet place and get some rest." [1]

And when I am refreshed, may I return to the crowds as an agent of his compassion—aware of the needs around me, caring deeply about those in pain, and becoming one who is willing to share in their suffering. In the *Compassionate Christ's* name I pray. Amen.

Meditation

The apostles have just returned from an extended preaching tour. Jesus had sent them out two by two. He had given them authority over evil spirits, instructed them to preach, cast out demons, and heal the sick.

Mission accomplished.

As they return, they're exhilarated but they're also exhausted. After their tour of duty, they're depleted, drained, spent, with nothing left to give. They have ministry fatigue.

"Please, no more preaching."
"No more people."
"No more problems."

But once you help one, five more follow you home. In a broken world, there seems to be no end to hurting people.

Jesus sees the circles under their eyes. He hears the growl in their stomachs. More importantly, he notices that their hearts are getting cold. The crowds have overwhelmed them—so many people, with so many problems, and there are so few to help. They've had enough. Jesus senses this and so he offers them an invitation.

> *"Then, because so many people were coming and going that they did not even have a chance to eat, he said to them, 'Come with me by yourselves to a quiet place and get some rest.' "* [2]

They try to sneak away by boat but a few in the crowd recognize them. These few each tell ten others, those ten inform hundreds, until thousands run along the shore and reach the other side of the lake ahead of the boat. The disciples see the multitude, they look at each other, raise their hands, shrug their shoulders, and say,

> *"So much for the quiet place. There goes the time of retreat and rest. I guess this means no nap and dinner."*

Even though the plan involved getting away from the crowd, Jesus doesn't see those who follow as an inconvenience or an interruption or even an irritation. They aren't spiritual stalkers who won't leave him alone. They're sheep without a shepherd, harassed and helpless, looking for someone who cares.

Jesus gets out of the boat and walks slowly through the crowd. Along the way, he stops and shows an interest in their lives. He listens to their questions and he gives answers. He touches them and he allows them to touch him. Halfway up the mountainside, he sits down and he begins to teach.

He doesn't say it directly but the crowd knows from the tone in his voice that he is intimately aware of each of their needs. Not only is he aware, he is willing to share in their sufferings. He is only one individual in the midst of the many, but the miracle of his compassion is that when he ministers to the masses, his little does much. His few words give many blessings.

By the time Jesus finishes teaching, it's late in the day. His disciples come to him worried and upset,

> *" 'This is a remote place,' they said, 'and it's already very late. Send the people away so they can go to the surrounding countryside and villages and buy themselves something to eat.'*
>
> *But he answered, 'You give them something to eat.' "* [3]

Jesus asks his disciples to become instruments of his compassion. But they look at the many and then they count their money and the two don't add up. Jesus sees them shaking their heads and so he asks them,

"How many loaves do you have? Go and see." [4]

They go on a search and report back,

"Five and two fish." [5]

He directs them to have all the people sit down on the grass. He takes the five loaves and the two fish, gives thanks, divides them among the disciples, and then tells them to give them to the people.

"They all ate and were satisfied, and the disciples picked up twelve basketfuls of broken pieces of bread and fish. The number of the men who had eaten was five thousand." [6]

The crowd is satisfied.
There's plenty left over.

The *Compassionate Christ* has taken little and done much.

[1]Mark 6: 31 [2]Mark 6:31 [3]Mark 6:35-37 [4]Mark 6:38 [5]Mark 6:38 [6]Mark 6:42-44

Reflection

What is compassion? In what way do you need Christ to display his compassion in your life?

Describe some of the moments in your life when you felt like a lamb without a shepherd—harassed and helpless?

Describe the seasons of your life when you viewed
the needs of people as an inconvenience, irritation,
or interruption.

In what part of your world is the *Compassionate Christ*
calling you to be an agent of his compassion? What is
your "little" that Christ wants to do "much" with?

Day Twelve:
The Determined Christ

Scripture Reading: Mark 8:27-9:1

Prayer

Father,

Your Son lived a determined life.

He told his disciples that he *must* go to Jerusalem. He *must* suffer many things and be rejected by the elders, chief priests, and teachers of the law. He *must* be killed and after three days he *must* rise again. This was his destiny!

> Satan couldn't deter him.
> Peter couldn't divert him.
> The pain of suffering couldn't dissuade him.

His redemptive love was decisive. It drove him to the cross to pay sin's penalty. It kept him on the cross until the penalty was paid. Finally, it lowered him from the cross, placed him in a tomb, and raised him three days dead declaring to the world that the payment was received in full.

During this day, I want to know the *Determined Christ*. I want to know the passion that he has for me, a passion so great that it would lead him to the cross. And when he calls me to come after him, empower me to live a determined life—may I deny myself, take up my cross, and follow him. It's in his name that I pray. Amen

Meditation

Peter got it half right.

He understood who Jesus was but he didn't understand what Jesus came to do. When Jesus asked, "Who do people say that I am?" some said that he was John the Baptist, or Elijah, or one of the prophets. But it was Peter who said,

"You are the Christ." [1]

He acknowledged that Jesus was the Messiah—the Son of God, and the Son of Man. He affirmed the dual nature and the one person of Christ. But when Jesus started to describe his work, Peter couldn't accept that.

> *"He then began to teach them that the Son of Man must suffer many things and be rejected by the elders, chief priests and teachers of the law, and that he must be killed and after three days rise again. He spoke plainly about this, and Peter took him aside and began to rebuke him."* [2]

Jesus made it clear that he had to go to Jerusalem.

The Son of Man *must* suffer many things.
    The elders, chief priests and teachers of the law *must* reject him.
    He *must* be killed and after three days rise again.

A divine *"must"* is driving him. His Father's eternal purpose is pushing him forward. Redemptive love is his resolve. He's determined to go to Jerusalem but Peter is just as determined to keep him away.

Peter takes Jesus aside and begins to rebuke him.

Suffering?

Rejection?

Crucifixion?

" 'Never, Lord!' he said. 'This shall never happen to you.' " [3]

Peter doesn't misunderstand Jesus; he disagrees with him. This isn't what Peter thought the Messiah should do.

"Pursuing and establishing physical kingdoms, power, and position, yes! That's the substance of the kingdom; not suffering, humiliation, and death."

But Jesus sees this deterrence for what it is—devil's work.

"But when Jesus turned and looked at his disciples, he rebuked Peter. 'Get behind me, Satan!' he said. 'You do not have in mind the things of God, but the things of men.' " [4]

Jesus knows that it is Satan who is at work in Peter. He's the one who is trying to distract him. He's the one who wants to keep him *away* from the cross, *away* from redemption, and *away* from victory.

Ironically, this same Satan will work through a different disciple, at another time, in an opposite way. Through Judas, he'll try and get Jesus *to* the cross, *to* the nails ... *to* death. If Satan can't distract him, he'll try and destroy him.

But it's the *Determined Christ*, not Satan, who is in control of his destiny. Jesus will go to the cross. But Satan isn't going to force him there. The elders, chief priests, and teachers of the law aren't going to lead him there. Rome won't march him there. He's determined to go to the cross on his own, driven only by love.

For the *Determined Christ*, there is no detour around the cross. He's going to and through it. He will march towards it; hang, suffer, and die on it; be taken down from it and on the third day rise again. For humanity's sake, there is no other way. With redemptive love, there is no wavering or wandering, no yielding or bending, no other options or choices.

His is the way of the cross.

The way of those who follow is the way of the cross. Jesus' call to discipleship is also a call to a determined life.

> *"Then he called the crowd to him along with his disciples and said: 'If anyone would come after me, he must deny himself and take up his cross and follow me. For whoever wants to save his life will lose it, but whoever loses his life for me and for the gospel will save it.' "* [5]

For Jesus, discipleship is about cross carrying. It's a daily call to death. But in that death there is also life, because the one who walks resolutely to the cross also walks, resurrected, out of the tomb.

He's determined.

Those who die with him will also rise with him. [6]

[1]Mark 8:27-29 [2]Mark 8:31-32 [3]Matthew 16:22 [4]Mark 8:33 [5]Mark 8:34-35 [6]Romans 6:4

Reflection

Do you consider yourself to be a disciple of Christ? If so, what does that mean?

Are you living a "determined" life? What type of "divine must" is driving your life?

What does it mean for you to "deny yourself, take up your cross and follow him"?

In what ways have you deterred Christ? How are you saying, "Never, Lord!"?

Day Thirteen:
The Prophetic Christ

Scripture Reading: Mark 13:1-37

Prayer

Father,

Your Son spoke plainly about the end of the age.

He prophesied times of deception, in which false Christs and false prophets would appear to try and deceive the elect. He foretold seasons of destruction. There would be wars, rumors of wars, famines, and earthquakes. He predicted that there would be persecution and distress; the glorious Jerusalem temple would be destroyed, brother would betray brother to death, and whoever was a Christ follower would be hated.

These signs were clues to his long awaited reappearance. While his own waited, he wanted to protect them, prepare them, and assure them of his presence. He prophesied in order that they might be on their guard, watch, and long for his coming.

During this day, and every day after, may I watch for the reappearance of the *Prophetic Christ*. And when I see the signs of the end of the age, may he remind me that the end is really just the beginning—a beginning, with him, for all eternity. It's in his name I pray. Amen.

Meditation

As the disciples left the temple mount, they looked up, stood in awe, and exclaimed how magnificent the house of God was. But the *Prophetic Christ* looked past the temple's past: past the building that Solomon had first built; past its destruction by the Babylonians; past the modest restoration by Zerubbabel; and past the magnificent and massive white stones of Herod the Great. He looked past the past, past the present, and prophesied into the future.

> " *'Do you see all these great buildings?' replied Jesus. 'Not one stone here will be left on another; every one will be thrown down.'* " [1]

Later, as Jesus sits on the Mount of Olives, opposite the temple, Peter, James, John, and Andrew come to him in private and ask,

> *"Tell us, when will these things happen? And what will be the sign that they are all about to be fulfilled?"* [2]

Again Jesus looks into the future. This time, he doesn't stop with the destruction of the temple. He fast forwards the prophecy and details the end of the age. He warns the disciples of deception, destruction, persecution, and distress.

> *"Watch out that no one deceives you."* [3]

> *"When you hear of wars and rumors of wars, do not be alarmed. Such things must happen but the end is still to come."* [4]

> *"All men will hate you because of me, but he who stands firm to the end will be saved."* [5]

"So be on your guard; I have told you everything ahead of time." [6]

The end of the age is going to bring the worst of times. But Jesus tells these things to his disciples to prepare them, not to frighten them. These horrible future seasons aren't going to be senseless, random acts of suffering. They're going to be signs. They're going to point to something beyond themselves, something yet to come, something imminent.

The worst of times will serve only as a precursor to the best of times. In these signs, Jesus is giving his followers inside information, clues to his coming.

"At that time men will see the Son of Man coming in clouds with great power and glory. And he will send his angels and gather his elect from the four winds, from the ends of the earth to the ends of the heavens." [7]

The *Prophetic Christ* is telling his disciples all that he knows ahead of time. He wants them to look for his reappearance, he wants them to be prepared, and he wants to protect them while they wait. He holds nothing back. He tells them everything—he will reappear, there will be signs, and he will come in the clouds with great power and glory.

The only thing he doesn't tell them is the day or the hour of his coming, and he doesn't tell them that because he doesn't know. Neither do the angels. Only the Father knows. One day the Father will say, "Now! Go! It's time!" Until then, the *Prophetic Christ* says to his followers, "Be on guard! Be alert! Watch!"

When Jesus speaks of the future, he doesn't fuel apocalyptic fears; he sparks faith. Fear dreads the end of the world; faith looks forward to the beginning of another world. One asks, "Where is God?" The other declares, "God is here! He's in the midst! Present always!"

The *Prophetic Christ* tells his disciples everything ahead of time so that they might be blessed.

> *"The revelation of Jesus Christ, which God gave him to show his servants what must soon take place. He made it known by sending his angel to his servant John, who testifies to everything he saw—that is, the word of God and the testimony of Jesus Christ. Blessed is the one who reads the words of this prophecy, and blessed are those who hear it and take to heart what is written in it, because the time is near."* [8]

Blessed are those who know the outcome of the end of the age because, at the end of the age, they know that it will all turn out right.

Blessed are those who are ready and waiting, on guard and alert, attentive to the signs, watching for the return of the Master, because, when he suddenly reappears, it might be a surprise but it won't be a shock.

Blessed are they who stand in awe of another temple.

"What massive stones! What magnificent buildings!" [9]

"They are before the throne of God and serve him day and night in his temple." [10]

[1]Mark 13:2 [2]Mark 13:4 [3]Mark 13:5 [4]Mark 13:7 [5]Mark 13:13 [6]Mark 13:23 [7]Mark 13:26-27 [8]Revelation 1:1-3 [9]Mark 13:1 [10]Revelation 7:15

Reflection

What signs of the end of the age do you see? Do they fuel fear or spark faith?

In what ways are you preparing for Christ's reappearance?

What comfort is there in knowing that the *Prophetic Christ* knows what's going to happen?

In what ways are you "on guard," "alert," "watching?"

Day Fourteen:
The Rejected Christ

Scripture Reading: Luke 4:14-30

Prayer

Father,

After your Son began his ministry in Galilee, he returned to his hometown of Nazareth. He wanted to let his family, friends, and neighbors know that the Messianic prophecies of the past were being fulfilled in the present—right then, right there, right in their own back yard.

He was the one who was sent to preach the good news, heal the sick, and release the oppressed. But the ones who knew him the best treated him the worst. His neighbors treated him as an outsider. His friends became enemies and the ones who had once played with him on the brow of the village hill tried to throw him off of it.

During this day, prepare me to receive the *Rejected Christ*. May my familiarity with him not cause contempt, or disdain, or defiance.

Today, open my heart to receive all that this Messiah would want to give. And if I am rejected in any way because of him, may the *Rejected Christ* open his arms and receive me. It's in his name I pray. Amen.

Meditation

There's nothing better than coming home. Unless, of course, those who are at home don't welcome you back!

After his temptation in the wilderness, Jesus had left his hometown of Nazareth and had gone to live in Capernaum on the north end of the Sea of Galilee. There, he began his ministry. During that time, he taught in their synagogues, he healed the sick, and he performed miracles. News about him spread rapidly throughout the whole countryside and everyone praised him.

Praise him? Not those in Nazareth.

When Jesus came home to Nazareth, he went to the Synagogue, as was his custom.[1] The attendant handed him the scroll of the prophet Isaiah. Jesus unrolled it until he found the Messianic prophecy in Isaiah 61:1-2. He paused for a moment and then he began to read.

> *"The Spirit of the Lord is on me,*
> *because he has anointed me*
> *to preach good news to the poor.*
> *He has sent me to proclaim freedom for the prisoners*
> *and recovery of sight for the blind,*
> *to release the oppressed,*
> *to proclaim the year of the Lord's favor."* [2]

After reading from the scroll, he rolled it back up, gave it to the attendant, sat down, and began to teach, saying,

> *"Today this Scripture is fulfilled in your hearing."* [3]

Jesus wants everyone who knows him—his friends and family, his neighbors, the one-time carpentry clients of his father's business—to know that the Messianic prophecies of the past are now being fulfilled in their presence. Right then, right there, right before their eyes, Isaiah's Messianic words have human flesh on them. Something good and glorious can and has come out of Nazareth.

But Jesus is too familiar to them to be the fulfillment of Messianic prophecy.

"Isn't this Joseph's son?" [4]

The ones that Jesus cares about most—members of his family, his childhood friends, those he went to worship with, those he worked with and played with—are the ones that he wants, more than any other, to receive his message. But the ones who know him don't want him. They don't just reject his message; they reject him.

By means of a proverb and references to Elijah's and Elisha's ministry to the Gentiles (and not to the house of Israel), Jesus rebukes his hometown for its unbelief. It's at this point that his homecoming turns into a lynching.

"All the people in the synagogue were furious when they heard this. They got up, drove him out of the town, and took him to the brow of the hill on which the town was built, in order to throw him down the cliff. But he walked right through the crowd and went on his way." [5]

A mob drives Jesus out of town. Along the way they yell, "Kill him! Throw him down the cliff!" But as they try to throw him off the hill, he—unhindered—turns away from the edge, steps forward, and then walks right through the crowd.

How he does it is a mystery. That he does it is a fact.

His time has not yet come. Only the Father will determine the time, the place, and the method of his death. For Jesus knows that there will be another hill, with another mob, that will be shouting another set of death chants,

"Crucify him! Crucify him!"

But on that hill they will not throw him down. Instead, he will allow them to raise him up. And when he is raised up, the Rejected Christ will say to the world,

"Though you reject me, I will not reject you."

> *"He was despised and rejected by men,*
> *a man of sorrows, and familiar with suffering.*
> *Like one from whom men hide their faces*
> *he was despised, and we esteemed him not.*
>
> *Surely he took up our infirmities*
> *and carried our sorrows,*
> *yet we considered him stricken by God,*
> *smitten by him, and afflicted.*
> *But he was pierced for our transgressions,*
> *he was crushed for our iniquities;*
> *the punishment that brought us peace was upon him,*
> *and by his wounds we are healed."* 6

1Luke 4:16 2Luke 4:18-19 3Luke 4:21 4Luke 4:22 5Luke 4:28-30 6Isaiah 53:3-5

Reflection

What's the difference between having a knowledge of Christ and being in an intimate relationship with Christ?

What does it feel like to be rejected? Rejected by the world you live in? Rejected by the family and friends you live with?

In what ways have you rejected Christ?

How has the *Rejected Christ* accepted you?

Day Fifteen:
The Willing Christ

Scripture Reading: Luke 5:12-26

Prayer

Father,

When a leper saw your Son, he ran to him, fell to his feet, and begged, "Lord, if you are willing, you can make me clean."[1] Your Son stretched out his hand, touched him, and said, "I'm willing. Be clean!" [2]

Through miracles, your Son demonstrated that he was not only able but also willing to help. He touched the untouchable, embraced the unacceptable, healed the incurable, did the unbelievable, and gave the unimaginable.

He was the man who was God. As the Son of Man, his heart was ready and willing. As the Son of God, his hand was ready and able.

During this day, give me a faith bold enough to run toward the *Willing Christ* so that I might plead,

"Lord, if you are willing, you can ...".

Make the words that I say a prayer and not a demand, a supplication and not an expectation, an appeal and not a claim. And as I ask for these things, may your will be done. It's in your Son's name I pray. Amen.

Meditation

Two men, a leper and a paralytic, desperately desire to get close to Jesus. The first shouldn't, the second can't. One is unclean and the other is unable. Whether unclean or unable, both are unwilling to stop until they are at the feet of Jesus.

Both decide to take a risk.

> They do what is socially unacceptable.
> They dare to do the unthinkable.
> They're undauntable.

They will get to Jesus' feet!

The leper is an "untouchable". He is isolated and separated because of his disease. Everywhere he goes he has to yell out, "Unclean! Unclean!" Leprosy has made him ceremonially unacceptable, socially unapproachable, physically undesirable, and emotionally unloved. He's a man who has to stay away and say to others as they pass by, "Danger! Don't touch!"

> *"The person with such an infectious disease must wear torn clothes, let his hair be unkempt, cover the lower part of his face and cry out, 'Unclean! Unclean!' As long as he has the infection, he remains unclean. He must live alone; he must live outside the camp."* [3]

But when the leper sees Jesus coming, he takes a risk. He can't stay away from him. Instead, he runs toward him. When he reaches Jesus, he falls with his face to the ground and begs him over and over again,

> *"Lord, if you are willing, you can make me clean."* [4]

The tone of his prayer isn't that of a demand,

"Make me clean!"

Nor is it an expectation,

"I'm believing that you will make me clean!"

Rather, it's a plea of surrender,

"If you are willing, you can make me clean."

The leper knows what Jesus is able to do; yet he doesn't claim or demand anything. Instead, he makes his plea known, surrenders the outcome, and lets Jesus decide.

Before Jesus *says* he's willing to heal him, he *shows* he's willing. He reaches out his hand, touches the "untouchable", and draws him close to himself. After the touch he says, "I'm willing. Be clean!" Immediately, the leprosy leaves him.

The paralytic isn't unclean but he is unable. However, unlike the leper, the paralytic has some friends. They carry him on his mat and try to get him into the house where Jesus is teaching. When they arrive and can't find a way to see Jesus because of the crowd, they, too, decide to take a risk. They go up on the roof of the house, tear off the ceiling tiles, and lower their friend on his mat into the middle of the crowd, right in front of Jesus.

The man's lips don't move. Neither do his legs. But in the stillness and the silence, there is a prayer, "Lord, if you are willing ...". When Jesus sees this, he says to the man lying helplessly at his feet,

"Friend, your sins are forgiven." [5]

But what's good news for one constitutes blasphemy for others.

> *"The Pharisees and the teachers of the law began thinking to themselves, 'Who is this fellow who speaks blasphemy? Who can forgive sins but God alone?'*
>
> *Jesus knew what they were thinking and asked, 'Why are you thinking these things in your hearts? Which is easier: to say, **Your sins are forgiven,** or to say, **Get up and walk?** But that you may know that the Son of Man has authority on earth to forgive sins ...' He said to the paralyzed man, 'I tell you, get up, take your mat and go home.' "* [6]

Which is easier: to heal a cripple or to cleanse a heart? Both are impossible for any mere man. But Jesus shows those in the house that he isn't just a man; he's also the Son of God. And so he does both—he heals the paralytic to show that he has power to heal as well as authority to forgive. In his humanity, Jesus is ready and willing to help; in his divinity, he's able.

As the paralyzed man takes up his mat and runs home—jumping and praising God—those in the house sit still, stunned, and dazed by what has just happened.

> *"Everyone was amazed and gave praise to God. They were filled with awe and said, 'We have seen remarkable things today.' "* [7]

Healing and forgiveness—these are the *Willing Christ's* "remarkable things".

---

[1]Luke 5:12 [2]Luke 5:13 [3]Leviticus 13:45-46 [4]Luke 5:12 [5]Luke 5:20 [6]Luke 5:21-24 [7]Luke 5:26

Reflection

What are you willing to risk to get at the feet of the *Willing Christ*?

In what areas of your life are you like the leper—unclean? In what areas of your life are you like the paralytic—unable?

Personalize and finish the prayer, "Lord, if you are willing you can ..."

How has the *Willing Christ* said to you, "Friend, your sins are forgiven!"? In what ways has he said, "Get up. Take your mat and go home."?

Day Sixteen:
The Forgiving Christ

Scripture Reading: Luke 7:29-50

Prayer

Father,

Your Son was accused of getting too close to sinners. The Pharisees—the spiritually "separated ones"; the self appointed spiritual enforcers of the law—labeled him a "glutton and a drunkard, a friend of tax collectors and sinners."[1] "Friend of tax collectors and sinners" he was, but not a "glutton" or a "drunkard."

He *did* eat, socialize, and talk with people who were on the outside looking in. He *did* get close to "sinners". But he got close in order to embrace those who thought they were outside the reach of love. He drew near so that he might surprise those who assumed they were past the point of mercy. He went to parties and social gatherings because he wanted to forgive those who believed they were beyond the grasp of grace.

During this day, I want to know that the *Forgiving Christ* has made me—a sinner—his friend. In the intimate moments of this day, show me the depth of his love. Reveal to me the price he paid for my forgiveness. Let me see, know, and feel how close he has come to me. And then, in joyful response, prompt me to bring something valuable to pour out at his feet. May this day be filled with the fragrance of that gift. It's in the *Forgiving Christ's* name I pray. Amen.

Meditation

The Pharisees had just accused Jesus of being a glutton and a drunkard. Yet one of them, Simon, invites him to his house for dinner. Jesus accepts. He goes to the Pharisee's house and reclines at his table.

> *"Now one of the Pharisees invited Jesus to have dinner with him, so he went to the Pharisee's house and reclined at the table. When a woman who had lived a sinful life in that town learned that Jesus was eating at the Pharisee's house, she brought an alabaster jar of perfume, and as she stood behind him at his feet weeping, she began to wet his feet with her tears. Then she wiped them with her hair, kissed them and poured perfume on them."* [2]

Simon is the one in the room who attaches the labels. He tags Jesus, "glutton, drunkard, friend of tax collectors and sinners". He brands the prostitute, "the woman who lives a sinful life in this town." But when it comes to himself, he proudly wears the badge of "Pharisee—a separated one."

Simon believes it's his self-appointed task to determine, decide, and discern others' levels of spirituality. He's designated himself spiritual prosecutor, judge, and jury. And so Simon's invitation goes well beyond asking Jesus to sit at his table; while he's sitting at his table, Simon is going to put Jesus on trial.

> *"When the Pharisee who had invited him saw this, he said to himself, 'If this man were a prophet, he would know who is touching him and what kind of woman she is—that she is a sinner.' "* [3]

Simon reasons that, if Jesus were a prophet, he would know what kind of woman is touching him, a sinner. In addition, if he were a prophet, he wouldn't let her touch him. Because he doesn't stop her from touching him, Simon concludes that Jesus isn't a prophet.

But Jesus knows what his host is thinking. He decides to go on the offensive and puts Simon on the stand. He begins his cross-examination by telling him a short story and closes it with a question.

> *"Two men owed money to a certain moneylender. One owed him five hundred denarii, and the other fifty. Neither of them had the money to pay him back, so he canceled the debts of both. Now which of them will love him more?"* [4]

The answer is obvious but Simon stumbles. He stumbles not because he doesn't know the answer but because he doesn't want to admit it.

> *"I suppose the one who had the bigger debt canceled."* [5]

The one with the bigger debt is sitting behind Jesus. When she entered the Pharisee's house, she ran to Jesus' feet; wet them with her tears; wiped them with her hair; kissed them; and then poured perfume on them. She filled the whole room with the fragrance of her love.

Somehow, somewhere, sometime in her recent past, Jesus had forgiven her. Like the fragrance locked in the alabaster jar, she had been set free. She had been given a new life and with that new life came the sweet bouquet of her devotion.

That's why she came.

When his grace washed over her past, her gratitude welled up in her eyes, poured down her cheeks and washed his feet. She's no longer "the woman who is living a sinful life" she is "the woman who *had lived* a sinful life".

Though her past is in her past, some—like Simon—won't let her forget it. Because they refuse to forget her past, Jesus gives Simon and those in the house something new to remember her by. He gives her a new name. He gives her a new title. He gives her a new label to describe her lavish act of love. He calls her,

"the woman who loves much." [6]

She has been forgiven much and so she loves much.

Jesus also gives Simon a new name. When he came to Simon's house, Simon refused to offer him any gesture of hospitality. He didn't offer any water for Jesus' feet. He gave no greeting, nor oil for Jesus' head. His inaction—everything he didn't do—demonstrated his disdain for Jesus. Jesus calls Simon,

"the one who loves little." [7]

The Pharisee stands condemned; the prostitute kneels forgiven. Simon had offered Jesus a backhanded, dubious, one-time invitation; but the prostitute had given him a forever-fragrant, costly expression of her devotion.

Grace had washed over her past.
Gratitude floods her present.

---

[1]Luke 7:34 [2]Luke 7:36-38 [3]Luke 7:39 [4]Luke 7:41-43 [5]Luke 7:43 [6]Luke 7:47
[7]Luke 7:47

Reflection

If you were labeled by your sin, what would people call you? (i.e. "the woman who had lived a sinful life in that town")

Because of the *Forgiving Christ*, what's your new name? (i.e. "the woman who loves much")

What are you willing to bring and pour out at the feet
of the *Forgiving Christ*. That which is fragrant and valuable or that which is left over?

How has grace washed over your past? How is gratitude
flooding your present?

Sabbath Day of Repentance

"The Pharisees and the teachers of the law who belonged to their sect complained to his disciples, 'Why do you eat and drink with tax collectors and 'sinners'?'

Jesus answered them, 'It is not the healthy who need a doctor, but the sick. I have not come to call the righteous, but sinners to repentance.' "

Luke 5:30-31

Repentance consists of two things: a confession of sin and a reception of grace. Neither stands alone. Both must occur.

> Without grace, a confession of sin
>   gets what it deserves—death.

> Without confession, grace
>   can't give what it desires—life.

Reflection

It what way are you a "sinner"? How are you spiritually sick and in need of the healing touch of Christ?

During the past sixteen days of your journey, how have you heard the forgiving voice of Christ? What words of grace has he spoken to you? How has he given you new life?

As you continue on this journey, what areas of your life would you like Christ to change?

Day Seventeen:
The Comforting Christ

Scripture Reading: Luke 12:1-34

Prayer

Father,

When a crowd of thousands surrounded your Son, he warned and then encouraged his disciples. He told them that en route to their heavenly destination, they would encounter hypocrisy, persecution, and earthly distractions—the most seductive of which would be greed.

He said, "Watch out! Be on your guard!" He also encouraged them. He compared his concern for the "little things" of this world (the worth of sparrows, the number of hairs on a head, the hunger of ravens, the beauty of lilies) to his consideration and provision for the "big things" (food, clothing, eternal life, the kingdom of God).

He said to them,

"Don't be afraid!"
"Don't worry!"

During this day, when I look at the birds of the air, the grass of the field, and all the other "little things" of my world, may the *Comforting Christ* reveal how much more he cares for me. It's in his name I pray. Amen.

Meditation

Clouds of sparrows dart over the massive crowd. They skim the ground for any morsel of food, set down, and then shoot back into the air. Thousands of people had run towards Jesus, but there was only room for a few hundred up front, near, close to him. Directly before him, seated at his feet, are the Twelve. But in between the feet of Jesus and the back of the crowd are the ones who are caught in the middle: the "trampled ones".

"Meanwhile, when a crowd of many thousands had gathered, so that they were trampling on one another, Jesus began to speak first to his disciples ..." [1]

With the massive crowd still undulating in front of him, Jesus steadies himself, turns to his disciples, and begins to speak. As the sea of people pulses, his words are steady and his voice is firm.

"Be on your guard against the yeast of the Pharisees, which is hypocrisy." [2]

"I tell you, my friends, do not be afraid of those who kill the body and after that can do no more." [3]

"Watch out! Be on your guard against all kinds of greed; a man's life does not consist in the abundance of his possessions." [4]

These are gale force warnings. The forecast for his disciples is certain. The sanctimonious winds of hypocrisy and false living are going to blow. Waves of persecution and painful living will break, froth, and rage. The currents of greed and the call to easy living will try to drag, tow, and suck them under.

These just aren't warnings; they're predictions.

But as he warns, he also comforts. It's one thing to predict a storm; it's another to calm it.

As he continues to teach, Jesus looks up and stares at the sparrows. His eyes dart as they shoot across the sky. He smiles. He turns and looks at the flowers in the field. He notes every color, distinguishing mark, and style. As he turns back to his disciples, he playfully picks a piece of hair off of Peter's shoulders. He squints, lifts it toward the light, and laughs.

Still holding the hair in his fingers, he stands up and lifts his hands to settle the swelling crowd. He wants them all to hear what he is about to say, especially the "trampled ones".

> *"Are not five sparrows sold for two pennies? Yet not one of them is forgotten by God. Indeed, the very hairs of your head are all numbered. Don't be afraid; you are worth more than many sparrows."* [5]

Jesus has an abiding concern for the "trampled ones": the ones who have fallen to the ground, the ones who have been pushed and walked over, the ones who have been shoved aside, the small ones, the weak ones, the insignificant ones, those of little social value, the ones who have been blocked from getting to the front, the ones that are far away from him. These are the ones who are worth more than many sparrows.

His Father has not forgotten any one of them. They are valuable, they are accounted for, and their needs are known. Jesus says, "No need to worry! Don't pull your hair out! For all of the hairs on your head are numbered."

Food? Clothing? Treasures in heaven? Again, Jesus calms and comforts the crowd. He places his provision for the "little things" next to his promise for the "big things". He sets the colorful wardrobe of wilting lilies beside the basic garments of daily life.

"Consider how the lilies grow. They do not labor or spin. Yet I tell you, not even Solomon in all his splendor was dressed like one of these. If that is how God clothes the grass of the field, which is here today, and tomorrow is thrown into the fire, how much more will he clothe you, O you of little faith!" 6

The *Comforting Christ* plots a logical course of reasoning for the turbulent crowd.

"If the Father thinks that five worthless sparrows are priceless, if he is able to count, know, and see one hair that falls from your head, if he takes the time to be the fashion designer for lilies, which last only a day, how much more will the Father care and provide for you?"

His Father's *"how much more"* is ...

Heard in a chirp,
Smelled in a lily and
Seen in a single fallen hair.
It's also seen on a cross.

On the cross, Jesus gives everything. He spares nothing. To all of the "trampled" ones he says,

"Don't be afraid! Don't worry!"

1Luke 12:1 2Luke 12:1 3Luke 12:4 4Luke 12:15 5Luke 12:6-7 6Luke 12:27-28

Reflection

In what way(s) do you feel like one of the "trampled ones"?

How has the *Comforting Christ* shown you that you are more valuable than the birds of the air or the lilies of the field?

What are the "little things" of your life? What are the "big things"?

In what area of your life do you need the *Comforting Christ* to say "Don't be afraid! Don't worry!"?

Day Eighteen:
The Longing Christ

Scripture Reading: Luke 13:22-35

Prayer

Father,

During his ministry, your Son taught primarily in the towns and villages of Galilee. He always knew, however, that he had to ultimately make his way to Jerusalem, the city that was known for killing the prophets and stoning those sent to it, the city of his lament and longing, the city of the cross.

As he hung on the cross, his beloved city ran from his embrace, recoiled from his touch, and rejected his affection. Even though he wept over her, she still was not willing. She who was first in his eyes became last and those who were last became first.

During this day, I pray that the *Longing Christ* would open his arms, gather me under his heavenly wings, and lead me through the narrow door into the house of the Father. May I take my place at the feast in the kingdom of God and sit next to all of his children, those from the east and west, the north and the south. It's in his name I pray. Amen.

Meditation

The city of Jerusalem is the summit of Jesus' ministry. It's the culmination of his redemptive climb. It's his destination: his goal.

On the peak of that city, he will stake a cross in the ground, ascend it, extend his hands in triumph, declare his victory, and—while high and lifted up—invite all people to share in his kingdom.

This invitation is meant for all but not all will come. Because of busyness and distraction, many will decline the invitation. Out of disinterest, some will dismiss it. And still others, unwilling to accept his Messianic claims, will discard it. Many are invited but few will come.

As Jesus makes his way to Jerusalem, a man asks,

"Lord, are only a few people going to be saved?" [1]

Jesus honors his question but gives an unexpected answer. He doesn't tell the man *how many* will be saved; instead, he tells him *who* will be saved.

"Make every effort to enter through the narrow door, because many, I tell you, will try to enter and will not be able to." [2]

The salvation door is narrow. There aren't many ways into the Father's house, there aren't unlimited opportunities, and there isn't even an unlimited amount of time. There's only one entrance into the house of God.

As Jesus goes to Jerusalem, he wants everyone to know that he's left the front door of his heavenly house wide open. He's the Door. There's no other entrance.

He's the one extending the invitation. He's the one

who longs to bring his entire family into his Father's house. It's his invitation and all are welcome.

As the Longing Christ walks to Jerusalem, he invites.
As he suffers, hangs on the cross, and dies, he
      invites.
As he rises from the dead, ascends, and waits for
      the day of his reappearance, he invites.

He is the one who holds the door open. But one day the door will close and—once that door is closed—it won't be opened again.

"Once the owner of the house gets up and closes the door, you will stand outside knocking and pleading, 'Sir, open the door for us.'

But he will answer, 'I don't know you or where you come from.'

Then you will say, 'We ate and drank with you, and you taught in our streets.'

But he will reply, 'I don't know you or where you come from. Away from me, all you evildoers!' " 3

Jesus explains to the crowd, that—upon judgment—the salvation door will be closed. After the door is closed, there will be those who will stand outside knocking and pleading with the *Longing Christ*, "Open the door for us." But the *Judging Christ* will say to them, "It's too late."

"There will be weeping there, and gnashing of teeth, when you see Abraham, Isaac and Jacob and all the prophets in the kingdom of God, but you yourselves thrown out. People will come from east and west and north and south, and will take their places at the feast in the kingdom of God. Indeed there are those who are last who will be first, and first who will be last." 4

With every invitation, there is always the possibility of rejection.

"Don't want it!"
"Don't need it!"
"Keep it to yourself!"

As the *Longing Christ* makes his way towards Jerusalem, he laments her spirit of rebellion. Throughout the centuries, she had killed the prophets and stoned the ones sent to her. In a short while when Jesus walks through her gates, she will refuse, resist, and reject him.

"*O Jerusalem, Jerusalem, you who kill the prophets and stone those sent to you, how often I have longed to gather your children together, as a hen gathers her chicks under her wings, but you were not willing!*" [5]

Though rejected, the *Longing Christ* holds open the door. Though his grace and mercy and peace are refused, he still offers. Though forgiveness is resisted, he still persists in extending nail-pierced hands. Day after day he invites. He welcomes those from every nation, from the east and the west, the north and the south. He holds the door open and says,

"Come on in!"
"You're invited!"
"There's a place just for you!"

[1]Luke 13:23 [2]Luke 13:24 [3]Luke 13:25-27 [4]Luke 13:28-30 [5]Luke 13:34

Reflection

What does it mean to enter through the "narrow door"?

What sense of urgency is there in knowing that one day the salvation door will be closed?

When the *Longing Christ* looks at your life, does he mourn?

In what ways does the *Longing Christ* want to gather you under his wings? Why would you or someone you know be unwilling to come?

Day Nineteen:
The Inviting Christ

Scripture Reading: Luke 14:1-24

Prayer

Father,

One Sabbath, your Son was invited to eat in the house of a prominent Pharisee. When he entered the house, he wasn't welcomed, but he was carefully watched. The invitation wasn't an invitation; it was a trap. But Jesus turned the trap into an opportunity to teach.

Through a healing, casual table talk and a parable, he taught about the urgency of compassion, the earthly rewards of humility, the eternal blessings of generosity, and the extension of the gospel to all people. And in the teaching he offered his own invitation. It wasn't a back-handed enticement, lure, or snare. His words were straight, sincere, and openhanded. He simply said,

"I'm having a banquet. You're all invited. When it's ready, I'll let you know. Please come!"

During this day, help me know that the *Inviting Christ* has requested my presence at his heavenly banquet. As I wait for the banquet call, may he give me a spirit of humility to take the "least important place", a heart of generosity to host a banquet for those who cannot repay, and an attitude of expectancy that longs for his call. It's in his name that I pray. Amen.

Meditation

Jesus knew the Sabbath invitation wasn't sincere, but he went anyway. As he entered the Pharisee's house, there in front of him—like live bait squirming in a concealed trap—was a man suffering from dropsy. The Pharisee had purposefully placed the man there. It was a predetermined, carefully planned, and premeditative act. As Jesus approached the man, the Pharisee and the experts in the law took their positions and carefully watched what Jesus would do.

Would he relieve suffering or rest on the Sabbath?
Would he fold his hands and pray or extend his
hands and heal?
Would he look on the man with pity or observe the
day with piety?

If Jesus heals the man, he breaks the Sabbath. If he keeps the Sabbath, he shatters the man. Which will it be: the sanctity of the person or the sanctity of the day?

Jesus makes his choice. He steps into the trap. As he does, he disarms it with a healing touch and a set of questions.

"Jesus asked the Pharisees and experts in the law, 'Is it lawful to heal on the Sabbath or not?' But they remained silent. So taking hold of the man, he healed him and sent him away.

Then he asked them, 'If one of you has a son or an ox that falls into a well on the Sabbath day, will you not immediately pull him out?' And they had nothing to say." [1]

The dinner invitation was a trap, but with the trap disarmed, Jesus begins to teach. As he makes his way to the table, he notices how the guests maneuver for the places of honor. Through a parable and some lively table talk, Jesus begins to explain banquet etiquette in the kingdom of God.

> *"But when you are invited, take the lowest place, so that when your host comes, he will say to you, 'Friend, move up to a better place.' Then you will be honored in the presence of all your fellow guests. For everyone who exalts himself will be humbled, and he who humbles himself will be exalted."* [2]

Humble yourself. Let someone else exalt you.

> *"But when you give a banquet, invite the poor, the crippled, the lame, the blind, and you will be blessed. Although they cannot repay you, you will be repaid at the resurrection of the righteous."* [3]

Give a banquet with great generosity.
Invite those who don't get invited to anything else.
Your reward will be at the resurrection.

When one of those at the table hears Jesus talking about these things, he exclaims,

> *"Blessed is the man who will eat at the feast in the kingdom of God."* [4]

Immediately, Jesus responds with a parable. In it, he describes the future celebration in the kingdom of God as well as those who will be invited, those who will refuse to come, and those who will attend.

In the parable, the host invites many to attend. They accept. But when it's time for the banquet to begin, all of those who were invited begin to make excuses. They refuse to come. They reject the host.

The host becomes angry. He wants his house to be full and so he invites the outcasts to come instead. His servants bring the poor, the blind, the crippled and the lame into his house. His house is finally full. The banquet begins. The doors are locked. The ones who refused the invitation stand outside without even a morsel from the banquet table.

The *Inviting Christ*, unlike the Pharisee, doesn't entrap nor does he entice. He simply invites. He has no ulterior motive. No hidden agenda. His guest list isn't exclusive; it's inclusive. All are welcome. He simply says, "Come! Be with me at my banquet!"

Receiving the invitation to the banquet is one thing; sitting at the table is another. Many are invited but few come. Between the banquet invitation and the first course there are countless excuses, refusals, and rejections.

And yet the *Inviting Christ* wants his house to be full. Before the doors close, he invites the outcasts, the nobodies, the insignificant, the unimportant, the inconsequential, and the ones who have been misused, used, and abused. In the kingdom of God, the man with dropsy is no longer a doorstop at the Pharisee's house; he's at the head table.

The Pharisee? He's locked outside begging for a crumb.

Jesus exalts the humble and humbles the exalted.

1Luke 14:3-6 2Luke 14:10-11 3Luke 14:13-14 4Luke 14:15

Reflection

Consider the man with dropsy. What does it feel like to be used, especially when you're suffering?

How could you practice the discipline of humility and take the "least important place" this day?

In what way can you throw a banquet for "the least" among you without expecting them to pay you back? What would be your resurrection reward?

Are you making any excuses for not attending the Great Banquet?

Day Twenty:
The Rejoicing Christ

Scripture Reading: Luke 15:1-32

Prayer

Father,

Wherever your Son went, he welcomed the social and sinful outcasts of his day. He didn't distance himself. He didn't push them away. He came near.

But the religious elite censured him for keeping good company with "bad company"; they criticized him for amassing a gathering of tax collectors; and they chastised him for seeking out, finding, and rejoicing over the return of "sinners".

The Pharisees wanted to distance themselves from "sinners". They wanted to be set apart. Undefiled. Your Son wanted to draw "sinners" near. He valued them. He searched until he found them and then he threw a party. He, and the whole company of heaven, celebrated their return.

During this day, I want to know the lengths to which the Rejoicing Christ went to find me. As I meditate on these things, show me the longing that was in his heart.

What thoughts came to his mind when he first realized that I was gone? Where did he look? How long did he search? What words did he call out as he ran after me? And when he found me, what kind of party did this *Rejoicing Christ* throw for me in heaven? Let me know these things this day. Amen

Meditation

The Pharisees and experts in the law are so close to the kingdom of God and yet they are so far away. They have the Prophets. They have the Messianic promises. And now, in Jesus, they have the fulfillment of both, right in front of them. He is so near to them and yet they stand at a distance: isolated, insulated, out of reach, and away from his touch.

The Pharisees live and die by their name. They are the "set apart ones". They believe that the "blessed man" stays away from "sinners".

> *"Blessed is the man*
> *who does not walk in the counsel*
> *of the wicked*
> *or stand in the way of sinners*
> *or sit in the seat of mockers." [1]*

In their eyes, Jesus isn't "blessed". Rather, he's the man who "sits in the seat of mockers, stands in the way of sinners, and walks in the counsel of the wicked." No wonder they mutter,

> *"Now the tax collectors and 'sinners' were all*
> *gathering around to hear him. But the Pharisees*
> *and the teachers of the law muttered, 'This man*
> *welcomes sinners and eats with them.' " [2]*

Jesus doesn't rebuke Pharisees. He doesn't debate them or raise his voice. Such reactions would only drive them away. Instead, he points to the sheep on the surrounding hills, he asks for a silver coin from the disciples' treasury, and he invites a father and his two sons to come and sit next to him. When the crowd is hushed and settled, Jesus tells them three successive stories.

> *"Suppose one of you has a hundred sheep and loses*
> *one of them. Does he not leave the ninety-nine in*

the open country and go after the lost sheep until he finds it?" 3

"Or suppose a woman has ten silver coins and loses one. Does she not light a lamp, sweep the house, and search carefully until she finds it?" 4

"There was a man who had two sons. The younger one said to his father, 'Father, give me my share of the estate.' So he divided his property between them.

Not long after that, the younger son got together all he had, set off for a distant country and there squandered his wealth in wild living." 5

In each story, something valuable is lost. The value of each loss dictates a diligent, urgent, and persistent search. In the course of time, the lost things are found, returned, or restored and an uproarious celebration ensues.

The greater the value of the item, the greater the loss; the greater the loss, the greater the urgency to search; and the greater the search, the greater the joy of recovery. In three parables, Jesus illustrates his love for the "lost things"; he depicts his determination to search until they are found; and he paints a portrait of the joy he has when they return home.

It's cause for a celebration.

"But we had to celebrate and be glad, because this brother of yours was dead and is alive again; he was lost and is found." 6

To those who recognize themselves as the lost sheep, the coin that has fallen to the ground, or the son who has left his father's house, these parables give new life. They resurrect the spiritually dead; they awaken deceased dreams; they rekindle numb and chilled relationships; and they revitalize and renew hope.

But even after the parables have been told, some in the crowd still want the *Rejoicing Christ* to stay away from the "sinners". The Pharisees and the experts in the law don't want anything to do with the celebration.

"The tax collector's sins are too great."
"The 'sinners' are too impure."
"Their immorality might be contagious."

"Celebrate? Not me. I'm staying away."

But Jesus doesn't stay away from anyone. He goes to the greedy, the guilty, and even, the so-called "godly". He gathers. He calls. He searches for those who have strayed, those who have slipped through the cracks of society, and those who have left home and made a mess of their lives.

And when he finds them, the *Rejoicing Christ* throws a party.

[1]Psalm 1:1 [2]Luke 15:1-2 [3]Luke 15:4 [4]Luke 15:8 [5]Luke 15:11-13 [6]Luke 15:32

Reflection

Describe what it feels like to be spiritually lost. If you can, describe what it feels like to be spiritually found.

In what ways have you wandered off from the flock, slipped through a crack in the floor, or left home and made a mess of your life?

What comfort does it bring to know that the *Rejoicing Christ* went looking for you?

What kind of party did the *Rejoicing Christ* throw when he found you?

Day Twenty-One:
The Tender Christ

Scripture Reading: Luke 18:1-17

Prayer

Father,

Your Son has strong hands. He raised his hands and storms were stilled. He opened his hands and thousands were fed. He stretched out his hands and the sick were healed and the dead were raised. Strong hands.

But your Son also has soft hands. He's the one who wipes the tears off the face of the widow. He's the one who bends down, forgives, and lifts up the spiritually broken. He's the one who calls the little children, sits them on his lap, and strokes their hair as he blesses them. Soft hands.

Into a tough world you gave to us a *Tender Christ*. When others look away from our plea, look down on our sin, or look past our need, your Son looks over us. He welcomes us like little children, extends his tender hand, and touches our lives with his justice, forgiveness, and blessing.

During this day, I want to experience the touch of the *Tender Christ*. As I struggle with an unfair adversary, I want to know the favorable fist of my Christ's justice. In the brokenness of my sin, I want to feel the caress of his grace. In the rebuke of the crowd, I want to see the welcoming wave of his blessing hand. It's in his name I pray. Amen

Meditation

A widow. A tax collector. Crying babies. They're different and yet they're the same. Though they're from different social classes, at different stages and ages of life, with different circumstances and needs—they're all the same. They're vulnerable.

> She's defenseless.
>> He's broken.
>>> And the babies are helpless.

Each of them needs the touch of the *Tender Christ*.

The widow needs the *Tender Christ's* favorable fist of justice. She's just lost a loved one. She's mourning. She's alone. Added to the grief and the loneliness is the burden of an adversary. Worse, she has no advocate. As she struggles with her adversary, no one stands next to her. No one speaks up for her. No one fights on her behalf.

> *"In a certain town there was a judge who neither feared God nor cared about men. And there was a widow in that town who kept coming to him with the plea, 'Grant me justice against my adversary.' "*[1]

The unjust judge looks away from the widow's plea. He doesn't care if some adversary is taking advantage of her. It's not his responsibility to be her advocate.

She cries, "Grant me justice!"

Annoyed, he orders, "Get her out!"

But when people have nowhere else to go, they don't go away. They stay put. They persist. They sit where they are until they are heard.

Finally, the judge grants her request. It's not because she's won him over but because she's worn him out. Jesus assures his disciples that if an unjust judge with a cast iron heart and an iron fist breaks down and gives justice to a persistent widow, how much more will the soft heart and the favorable fist of the Father bring about justice?

> *"And will not God bring about justice for his chosen ones, who cry out to him day and night? Will he keep putting them off? I tell you, he will see that they get justice, and quickly."* [2]

The tax collectors of the world need the *Tender Christ's* caress of grace. For the tax collector, the exposure of his sin brings humiliation, brokenness, and alienation. Others stand upright in the temple, praying pious prayers and pointing to him as an example of what they are not. As they look at him, they look down.

> *"Two men went up to the temple to pray, one a Pharisee and the other a tax collector. The Pharisee stood up and prayed about himself: 'God, I thank you that I am not like other men—robbers, evildoers, adulterers—or even like this tax collector. I fast twice a week and give a tenth of all I get.'"* [3]

But the *Tender Christ* will not break this "bruised reed" and he will not blow out this "smoldering wick".[4] Instead, he binds up and ignites. The tax collector's cry for mercy is answered with the tender touch of grace. Once he was the downcast one in the corner, standing at a distance, humiliated and broken over his sin. Now, he is the exalted one, lifted up by the hand of grace.

The babies and children of the world need the *Tender Christ's* welcoming wave. They're the helpless ones and needy ones. They're the littlest. Because they're the littlest, they tend to get looked over in a crowd. The world assumes that the biggest people have the biggest needs and the littlest people have the littlest needs. In a crowd, where there is an important man and eternal things being discussed, the disciples think that there is no time for these little ones. After all, the little ones make the biggest mess, they generate the greatest amount of noise, and they require the largest amount of work.

> *"People were also bringing babies to Jesus to have him touch them. When the disciples saw this, they rebuked them. But Jesus called the children to him and said, 'Let the little children come to me, and do not hinder them, for the kingdom of God belongs to such as these. I tell you the truth, anyone who will not receive the kingdom of God like a little child will never enter it.' "* [5]

The *Tender Christ* doesn't want the little ones to be kept away. He waves his hand, welcomes them with a smile, open arms, and pats on their heads. As they come, he blesses them.

The kingdom belongs to the "little ones".

When the world looks away from the pleas of a widow, looks down on the sin of a tax collector, or looks past the needs of the "littlest ones", the *Tender Christ* responds. He reaches down, opens his hand, and gives a tender touch.

His fist is justice.
His caress is forgiveness.
His touch is blessing.

---

[1]Luke 18:2-3 [2]Luke 18:7-8 [3]Luke 18:10-12 [4]Isaiah 42:3 [5]Luke 18:15-17

Reflection

In what way have you been treated like the widow? How have people looked the other way and left you defenseless?

In what way have you been treated like the tax collector? How have people looked down on you because of your sin and left you without grace?

In what way have you been treated like the little children? How have people looked past you and left you helpless?

How has the *Tender Christ* touched your life with justice? Forgiveness? Blessing?

Day Twenty-Two:
The Attentive Christ

Scripture Reading: Luke 18:35–19:10

Prayer

Father,

Wherever your Son walked, a crowd followed. He was constantly surrounded by a mass of people. Though he was always in the middle of the multitudes, somehow he never lost sight of the importance of the individual.

As he walked through Jericho, two men wanted to see him but neither could. Bartimaeus, the blind beggar, was sightless. Zacchaeus, the chief tax collector was short and out of sight. But Jesus saw them both. He stopped. He heard the cry of the blind beggar over the shouts of the crowd and he saw the short man perched in a tall sycamore tree. He was attentive. He noticed the need that others ignored. He heard the cries that others blocked out. He saw what others missed.

During this day, when the world passes me by, I need to be assured that the *Attentive Christ* notices me. Remind me that he stops, picks me out of the crowd, and gives me his full attention.

When he asks, "What do you want me to do for you?" may I, in faith, declare the desire that beats fast within my heart. And when he says, "I must stay at your house today" may I welcome him knowing that Salvation will be the guest of honor. Amen.

Meditation

As Jesus approaches Jericho, a blind beggar named Bartimaeus sits by the roadside. He's at his usual spot, at his usual time. He knows the usual flow of people and the stream of their schedule. He's always known the darkness and he's adapted. His routine and the regular comings and goings of his town have given him a sixth sense of control. But today's current is unusual.

There's a different rush in the crowd. This surge is larger than any he's known and the noise is cresting as it approaches. Something new is happening, someone new is coming to his town, and somehow he's got to figure out what's going on.

> *"When he heard the crowd going by, he asked what was happening. They told him, 'Jesus of Nazareth is passing by.'*
>
> *He called out, 'Jesus, Son of David, have mercy on me!'*
>
> *Those who led the way rebuked him and told him to be quiet, but he shouted all the more, 'Son of David, have mercy on me!' "* [1]

Just because he's blind doesn't mean he can't see. Before the crowd beholds the Messiah, he perceives that this Jesus is the "Son of David." He knows that he is the Son of God. He envisions this man to be the "Servant of the Lord" that Isaiah prophesied about, the one who was a "light to the Gentiles" the one that would "open eyes that are blind", and "release from the dungeon those who sit in darkness." [2]

He "sees" … and shouts all the more!

Above the roar of the crowd, Jesus hears the beggar's supplication. He hears his cry and his creed. He stops and orders the man to be brought to him. Jesus gives him his full attention and asks,

> " 'What do you want me to do for you?'
>
> 'Lord, I want to see,' he replied.
>
> Jesus said to him, 'Receive your sight; your faith has healed you.' " [3]

Bartimaeus prays, "Lord, let my eyes see what my heart believes." His prayer is answered. The Messiah he saw only by faith, he now sees in the flesh.

Zacchaeus is short in stature, short in morals, short on friends, but he is big on ambition. He's become the little big man of Jericho. As the region's chief tax collector, he's taxed his way to the top. But all of his money can't buy him a front row seat as Jesus passes by.

Using the ingenuity that comes from being a small man in a big man's world, he runs ahead of the crowd, climbs a sycamore tree, and waits for Jesus to pass by. He's determined to see Jesus. He will have the best view. Best of all, he won't have to deal with the big man's crowd; he'll be above it, not underneath it.

> "When Jesus reached the spot, he looked up and said to him, 'Zacchaeus, come down immediately. I must stay at your house today.' So he came down at once and welcomed him gladly.
>
> All the people saw this and began to mutter, 'He has gone to be the guest of a **sinner**.' " [4]

Jesus wants to see Zacchaeus more than Zacchaeus wants to see him. Jesus stops, looks up, sees the little man with the big chip on his shoulder perched in the sycamore tree. He tells him to come down immediately and says, "I must stay at your house today."

It's the *Attentive Christ* who picks little Zacchaeus out of the crowd. He chooses the chief tax collector, the short one, and the one known to the crowds as "sinner".

The crowd swells with resentment. The people mutter. They grumble. They shake their heads because they know that this little man is a big cheat. But something big has just happened to this little man. The chip is no longer on his shoulder. Salvation has come to his house.

> *"But Zacchaeus stood up and said to the Lord, 'Look, Lord! Here and now I give half of my possessions to the poor, and if I have cheated anybody out of anything, I will pay back four times the amount.' "* [5]

As the world whirls, no one listens, no one looks, and no one cares about Bartimaeus and Zaccheus. They're lost in the crowd. But the *Attentive Christ* stops, takes note, and is aware of the "lost one" in the midst of the many.

> *"For the Son of Man came to seek and to save what was lost."* [6]

[1]Luke 18:36-39 [2]Isaiah 42:6-7 [3]Luke 18:41-42 [4]Luke 19:5-7 [5]Luke 19:8 [6]Luke 19:10

Reflection

How has the world passed you by? How has it ignored your cry for help?

If the *Attentive Christ* were to ask, "What do you want me to do for you?" what would be your answer?

What are you willing to do to see/to be seen by Jesus?

How has the *Attentive Christ* picked you out of the crowd?

Sabbath Day of Response

"Then I heard the voice of the Lord saying, 'Whom shall I send? And who will go for us?'

And I said, 'Here am I. Send me!'"

Isaiah 6:8

Grace is God taking the initiative. He acts. He moves. He invites. He works. He changes lives. He seeks and he saves.

Following right behind grace is a response.

Grace is the gift.
Response is the thrill on the face when the gift is opened.

Grace changes everything you know about your world.
Response lets the world know that everything about you has changed.

Grace saves and then asks—"Who will go?"
Response waves its hands and answers—"Send me!"

Reflection

How has God taken the initiative in your life?

How has Christ's grace changed everything in your world?

Before you continue on your journey, list some of the ways you could respond to the grace of Christ.

Day Twenty-Three:
The Incarnate Christ

Scripture Reading: John 1:1-18

Prayer

Father,

The mystery of your divinity is that before time began, eternity existed, before humanity there was solely Trinity, and before the world's drama took the stage, there was only one story: the story of your Son, the Word. He had no beginning, no end; he was, is, and will forever remain as *"Always."*

Because he was the Word, he couldn't remain mute, he wouldn't remain hushed or silent, he had to speak. From eternity he said, "Let there be ...". He fashioned everything from nothing.

He created time and then he entered it. The Eternal Word spoke to his creation. He used its language and heard its cry. He took on human flesh. He became incarnate. Eternity wrapped itself in time. *"Always"* became *"every day"* in every way. The Word became a man. He made divinity touchable, approachable, and knowable.

During this day, I want the *Incarnate Christ* to come near to me. Though he may be absent to my meager eye, assure me that he is present, physically, by my side. I want to touch him. I need to bow before him. I want to ask him, with great confidence and boldness, for the fullness of his grace and truth. Above all, I desire to know him and—through him—to see you, Father. It's in his name I pray. Amen.

Meditation

Every story starts somewhere.

Either it opens with a fanciful, "Once upon a time ...", or it launches out with an adventurous, "A long time ago ...", or it looks back, reminisces, and recollects past events with a nostalgic, "I remember when ...". But what do you do when the story you're about to tell has no beginning?

It has no beginning because the one you're telling the story about is eternal. He's beyond time, before time, between times. His story is the never beginning story but it's also the never-ending story. Where do you begin when there is no beginning? Such is the dilemma of the apostle John.

As he's about to start his Gospel—the story of the Eternal Word, the Son of God, who wraps himself in human flesh—he writes a prologue. He tells a pre-story before he speaks of history. He describes the Eternal Word before that Word became flesh, before he became Jesus.

> *"In the beginning was the Word, and the Word was with God, and the Word was God. He was with God in the beginning.*
>
> *Through him all things were made; without him nothing was made that has been made. In him was life, and that life was the light of men. The light shines in the darkness, but the darkness has not understood it."* [1]

Mystified, John says,

> "*Before* it all began the Word was there."
> "*When* it all began he was there."
> "*After* it began he was there."

John's pre-story takes place in eternity. It's beyond the capacity of human reason and is filled with mystery. But the good news that John declares is that the Eternal Word doesn't want to remain a mystery.

He wants to be known. He wants to reveal himself. He wants to speak. He wants to move from pre-story to human history, unknown to known, invisible to visible, distant to near. He wants to become the *Incarnate Christ*. He wants to take on human flesh and be called "Jesus".

> *"He came to that which was his own, but his own did not receive him. Yet to all who received him, to those who believed in his name, he gave the right to become children of God—children born not of natural descent, nor of human decision or a husband's will, but born of God.*
>
> *The Word became flesh and made his dwelling among us. We have seen his glory, the glory of the One and Only, who came from the Father, full of grace and truth."* [2]

The *Incarnate Christ* pitches his tent on human soil. He walks among those he created. He dwells with them, he speaks to them, he listens to their cry, he feels their pain, and he comes to their aid. He is close—so close—always present. And as the *Incarnate Christ* comes, he doesn't come empty handed. His hands are full of grace and truth. He brings blessing after blessing after blessing—heavenly gifts for earthly grief.

"From the fullness of his grace we have all received one blessing after another. For the law was given through Moses; grace and truth came through Jesus Christ. No one has ever seen God, but God the One and Only, who is at the Father's side, has made him known." [3]

The distinguishing characteristic of the incarnation is that the *Incarnate Christ* takes the initiative. The One and Only leaves the Father's side and becomes the man called Jesus. As a man, he makes divinity touchable, approachable, and knowable.

The definitive challenge of the incarnation is not to comprehend *how* God did it or to understand *why* he did it. Instead, it involves living in the reality *that* he did it. The *Incarnate Christ* is still physically present. He hasn't moved out of the neighborhood.

As Grace he forgives.
As Truth he reveals.
As the One and Only, he's still the only one who reveals the Father.

[1]John 1:1-5 [2]John 1:11-14 [3]John 1:16-18

Reflection

What comfort is there in knowing that your God took on human flesh?

How has the *Incarnate Christ* "made his dwelling among you"? How is Jesus' story living and active in you?

The *Incarnate Christ* is "full of grace and truth". As Grace, how has he forgiven you? As Truth, what has he revealed to you? How have you received "one blessing after another"?

What does it mean that the One and Only is the only one that reveals the Father?

The Sacrificial Christ

Scripture Reading: John 1:19-51

Prayer

Father,

Generation after generation after generation waited in anticipation for the advent of the Messiah, your Son made flesh. They longed for his coming. They looked for his arrival. When he tarried, they gripped ever tighter the Messianic promises given to them by Moses and the Prophets. That he would come was a fact. When he would come was a mystery. Who he would be—the Scriptures were full of clues.

John the Baptist found a number of those clues and began to unravel the Messianic mystery. Father, when he baptized Jesus, you spoke, the Spirit descended, and both of you affirmed the divinity of the carpenter's son. No more guessing, no more wondering, no more hoping. Jesus is the Messiah. And so John pointed to Jesus and declared, "Look, the Lamb of God! He is the *Sacrificial Christ* who takes away the sins of the world."

During this day, help me live in the reality of full forgiveness. Remind me that the *Sacrificial Christ* suffered and died instead of and in place of me. Assure me that the sacrifice of the Lamb of God was not only universal but also personal. He died for the world but he also died for me. In his name I pray. Amen.

Meditation

Between a promise and its fulfillment is a waiting room.

John the Baptist, his disciples, and an entire generation of Jews have been sitting in that room and now the
door is about to be opened. They have read the
Scriptures, they understand the characteristics of the
Christ, they know the marks of the Messiah, but they
don't have any candidates.

Many had thought John the Baptist was the Christ but
he denied the title.

> *"Now this was John's testimony when the Jews of
> Jerusalem sent priests and Levites to ask him who
> he was. He did not fail to confess, but confessed
> freely, 'I am not the Christ.'*
>
> *John replied in the words of Isaiah the prophet, 'I
> am the voice of one calling in the desert, 'Make
> straight the way for the Lord.' ' "* [1]

John understands his part in this divine drama. He is
the one who is supposed to get the path ready. No
upstaging. No grandstanding. No seeking the spotlight.
At the appointed time, his role is to roll out the Messianic
carpet, straighten it, signal the trumpets, and announce
the arrival of the Anointed One: the Christ. And when he
sees the carpenter's son, Jesus of Nazareth, that's exactly what he does.

> *"The next day John saw Jesus coming toward him
> and said, 'Look, the Lamb of God, who takes away
> the sin of the world! This is the one I meant when I
> said, 'A man who comes after me has surpassed me
> because he was before me.' ' "*[2]

John calls Jesus the Lamb of God. The priests and the Levites who were sent from Jerusalem to question him know exactly what he is trying to say. That name isn't just a title; it infers atonement, redemption, sacrifice. And every Jew knows the stories about the sacrificial lamb.

They all know the story about the ram caught in the thicket. They all remember how God tested Abraham and told him to sacrifice his only son, the son of promise, Isaac. They know about the knife, the wood, and the fire. They held their breath when Abraham tied up Isaac, placed him on the altar, raised his hand, and made ready to slay his son. They breathed a sigh of relief when the angel said "stop" and Abraham saw the lamb caught in the thicket.

> *"Abraham looked up and there in a thicket he saw a ram caught by its horns. He went over and took the ram and sacrificed it as a burnt offering instead of his son."* [3]

They all know the story about the Passover Lamb.

> *"The blood will be a sign for you on the houses where you are; and when I see the blood, I will pass over you. No destructive plague will touch you when I strike Egypt."* [4]

They all know the requirements of the sacrificial system. Whether it is a burnt offering, a sin offering, or a guilt offering, the sacrifice has to be a pure lamb.

> *"When a person commits a violation and sins unintentionally in regard to any of the Lord's holy things, he is to bring to the Lord as a penalty a ram from the flock, one without defect and of the proper value in silver, according to the sanctuary shekel. It is a guilt offering."* [5]

In one sentence, John declares who the Messiah is, what he's come to do, and what he has to offer.

> *"Look, the Lamb of God, who takes away the sin of the world."* [6]

This Jesus of Nazareth is substitute. He is sacrifice. He is sin offering. As the *Sacrificial Christ*, he is pure, spotless, and undefiled. He is the sum of all sacrificial lambs. As the Lamb of God, this priceless gift from heaven has come to forfeit his life on behalf of sinful humanity.

God's Son comes to die instead of and in place of the world that rejects him. The *Sacrificial Christ* comes to buy back his world. He redeems it with his own blood. It's his blood on the doorpost, his blood on the altar of sacrifice, and his blood on the cross. From the cross, he declares,

> "I take away the sins of the world!"

---

[1]John 1:19-20,23 [2]John 1:29-30 [3]Genesis 22:13 [4]Exodus 12:13 [5]Leviticus 5:15 [6]John 1:29

Reflection

John the Baptist described Jesus as, "the Lamb of God, who takes away the sin of the world". How does that affect they way you think about Christ?

What's the difference between knowing that "the *Sacrificial Christ* died for the world" and knowing that "the *Sacrificial Christ* died for you"?

The *Sacrificial Christ* died "instead of you" and "in place of you". How does that change your life?

Consider the atoning work of the *Sacrificial Christ*. What sets Christianity apart from all other religions?

Day Twenty-Five:
The Passionate Christ

Scripture Reading: John 2:1-25

Prayer

Father,

When your Son became a man, he took upon himself all that is humanity. During long nights, his eyes became bloodshot and they cried for sleep. After long days, his muscles cramped and his body ached. In between the nights and the days, his stomach growled, his throat burned, and his feet hurt.

He was born, he lived, and he died. Physically, he was like us. But he also had emotions—intense emotions. He knew great joy and experienced great sorrow. He was driven forward by passion and slowed down by compassion. He felt the rage of anger and the rest that comes with peace. Emotionally, he was like us. The good news is that the *Passionate Christ* not only acts on our behalf but, when he acts, it is with the force of emotion.

During this day, help me believe that this *Passionate Christ* has intense emotions for me. Show me the intensity of his love, the zeal of his grace, and the fire of his purpose for my life.

And when I stray, let me hear him weeping, let me see his pain, and let me know the grief behind his all-consuming longing. It's in his name I pray. Amen.

Meditation

A wedding is a gala affair: festive, full of joy, short on worries, and long on well wishes. It's a community event that could last up to a week. In a close-knit village like Cana, everyone is invited. It's a time to celebrate and Jesus is right in the center of it all, dancing, laughing, and carrying on. This isn't a time to deliver a sermon; it's a time to dance with the bride. He discerns the moment and the moment Jesus discerns is joy. And so he dances. He dances into the night. He dances until his mother pulls him aside.

She scurries him away from the celebration and hurries him around to the back of the house. She points to the jars in front of him, shrugs her shoulders and says, "They have no more wine." [1]

No more wine.

To end the celebration before it's over is not only a social embarrassment, it's a serious communal offense. This isn't any way for a couple to start its life together. The wine may be gone, but Jesus isn't ready for the celebration to be over, not now, not like this. Jesus orders the servants to fill six stone jars with water. They do. He tells them to take some of the water and bring it to the master of the banquet.

> *"They did so, and the master of the banquet tasted the water that had been turned into wine. He did not realize where it had come from, though the servants who had drawn the water knew. Then he called the bridegroom aside and said, 'Everyone brings out the choice wine first and then the cheaper wine after the guests have had too much to drink; but you have saved the best till now.' "* [2]

Jesus honors the bridegroom, he keeps the wedding

reception going, and he saves the best till last. The *Passionate Christ* has a zeal for joy and is consumed with celebration.

Later, Jesus visits another house: his Father's house in Jerusalem. This house is different than the one in Cana. It doesn't welcome guests to a wedding; rather, it welcomes them to worship.

Wedding and worship. Both are a celebration, both are supposed to be full of joy, both have a groom and a bride, both are to be filled with dancing. [3]

Yet when Jesus enters his Father's house, he finds it desecrated. Commercialism consumes the courtyard. A passion for profit replaces the singing of psalms of praise. The front door of his Father's house was left open and a den of thieves had taken up residence.

> *"In the temple courts he found men selling cattle, sheep and doves, and others sitting at tables exchanging money. So he made a whip out of cords, and drove all from the temple area, both sheep and cattle; he scattered the coins of the moneychangers and overturned their tables. To those who sold doves he said, 'Get these out of here! How dare you turn my Father's house into a market!'*
>
> *His disciples remembered that it is written: 'Zeal for your house will consume me.' "* [4]

His emotions are intense. His actions are premeditated. As his righteous indignation builds, passion and purpose intertwine. He fashions a whip out of cords. He snaps it into the air to silence the crowd. He flails the whip back and forth, driving the sheep and cattle out of the temple area. As he approaches the tables of the moneychangers, he takes the butt of the whip and scatters the neatly stacked piles of coins and then—for good measure—he overturns their tables.

With whip still in hand, he moves towards those who sell the doves. He doesn't coo or speak in soft murmurs. Today he's a hawk, not a dove. He points to the doves and then lashes out at their dealers, "Get these out of here! How dare you turn my Father's house into a market!" [5]

Zeal for his Father's house consumes him.

The *Passionate Christ* is a God of intense emotion. He experiences the full range of human feelings. He knows extreme joy and fierce anger.

He doesn't just attend a wedding; he's the life of it. He celebrates, revels, and laughs. When he enters his Father's house, zeal consumes him. He cleanses, rebukes, and lashes out.

Passion drives him. Compassion guides him. When he acts, he acts with the full force of emotion. When this Jesus loves, he just doesn't love; he falls in love.

     Madly.
       Deeply.
         Passionately.

[1]John 2:3 [2]John 2:8-10 [3]Psalm 149:3 [4]John 2:14-17 [5]John 2:16

Reflection

How does the reality that the *Passionate Christ* has intense emotions change the way you view God?

What does it mean that the *Passionate Christ* acts out of the full force of love, or jealousy, or anger?

What type of emotion do you need the *Passionate Christ* to express in your life?

The *Passionate Christ* just doesn't love you; he's in love with you. How does that affect your relationship with him?

Day Twenty-Six:
The Loving Christ

Scripture Reading: John 3:1-21

Prayer

Father,

Your Son, the Word made flesh, is a poem of love. From eternity, you sent Poetry into motion, out of heaven and down to earth. The virgin conceived your Verse of love; she enveloped him in flesh and delivered him to the world. At the proper time, the envelope was opened, the contents read, and the courtship began. The poem started,

> "Beloved,
>   For God so loved the world ..."

They were the words of a salvation song: a sonnet. Through a redemptive rhyme scheme, the Lover wooed, romanced, and pursued his Beloved. But she resisted, rejected, and rebuffed his love. And so to prove his love authentic and his intentions pure, he climbed the highest hill, opened his arms wide, and cried, "I love you". He sealed his intentions with a kiss: a kiss from the cross. In love, he finished the sonnet, breathed his last, and signed his name with the red rose of his blood,

> "With love! From here to eternity,
>   Jesus, the Lover of your soul."

During this day, I want to know that the *Loving Christ* not only loves the world but that he's in love with me. Help me see all the ways that he is trying to woo me. Let me hear the redemptive rhyme, the poetry, the verse, and the sonnet of his salvation. I pray this as the Beloved who longs for the Lover. Amen.

Meditation

Nicodemus, a man of the Pharisees and a member of the Jewish ruling council, is a bright man and yet he's spiritually in the dark. He's Israel's teacher and yet he's looking for the truth. The number of his years makes him cautious but the number of Jesus' miracles makes him curious.

> *"He came to Jesus at night and said, 'Rabbi, we know you are a teacher who has come from God. For no one could perform the miraculous signs you are doing if God were not with him.'*
>
> *In reply Jesus declared, 'I tell you the truth, no one can see the kingdom of God unless he is born again.' "* [1]

Born again?

For a settled, old Pharisee this is an unsettling, new proposition. Physically, it's inconceivable. Spiritually, it's incomprehensible. Practically, it's impossible. Though he breathes the air he can't see without laboring, Nicodemus can't seem to inhale this new breath of life. The very thought of a second birth takes his breath away. Conceived in divine love, that's a miracle. Born of God, that's a mystery. Delivered and called a child of God, that's amazing. How can this be?

> *"You should not be surprised at my saying, 'You must be born again.' The wind blows wherever it pleases. You hear its sound, but you cannot tell where it comes from or where it is going. So it is with everyone born of the Spirit.*
>
> *'How can this be?' Nicodemus asked."* [2]

His question is both practical and personal.

"How does it happen?
Why does it occur?
When? Where?"

But between the words, in the subtext, dwelling beneath his question is a deeper question. He's wondering, "Could this second birth be *for me?* Does God *love me?*" It's a personal question and yet the *Loving Christ* gives Nicodemus a universal answer. He gives a universal answer because it's a universal question. The whole world wonders, "Does God *love me?*" Nicodemus isn't the only one who is in the dark. To all of those who have loved and lost, or never loved at all, the *Loving Christ* opens his heart and says:

> *"For God so loved the world that he gave his one and only Son, that whoever believes in him shall not perish but have eternal life. For God did not send his Son into the world to condemn the world, but to save the world through him."* [3]

In Jesus, divinity falls in love with humanity. The Word made flesh woos his Beloved with extravagant acts of love. His love is selfless, sacrificial, and not overly sentimental. Everything he does is an expression of an otherworldly love. It's a love of another kind, from another place, for another reason.

He comes to rescue his Beloved. He doesn't come to condemn her. To a sleeping beauty, dead in her sin but alive in his heart, his love brings the kiss of life. The stroke of his hand on her hair is that of grace. As she wakes, he—the Lover—promises his Beloved that they will live, not just happily ever after, but eternally ever after.

For Nicodemus, this is no fairy tale. This love story is real. This love story is for him. The *Loving Christ* said that he loved the whole world but Nicodemus knew that the *Loving Christ* couldn't possibly do that without loving him, too.

Later, on the darkest day of history—the day the world killed the *Loving Christ*—Nicodemus stepped out of the shadows and shined his own light of love.

> *"Later, Joseph of Arimathea asked Pilate for the body of Jesus. Now Joseph was a disciple of Jesus, but secretly because he feared the Jews. With Pilate's permission, he came and took the body away. He was accompanied by Nicodemus, the man who earlier had visited Jesus at night. Nicodemus brought a mixture of myrrh and aloes, about seventy-five pounds."* [4]

For one who was once in the dark, Nicodemus' love burns bright. He comes and cradles Jesus. He carries the extinguished Light of the World to the tomb. He anoints the *Loving Christ* with a mixture of myrrh and aloes. Every action, every step, every word is a testimony of his love. It's a newborn love. It flames with passion and says to a dark world,

"This man loved and died *for me!*"

[1]John 3:2-3 [2]John 3:7-9 [3]John 3:16-17 [4]John 19:38-39

Reflection

Are there any shadows that you are hiding in? Are you afraid to be seen with Jesus or afraid that Jesus might see you?

Describe life ...
    in the shadows/out of the shadows
    in the light/in the darkness

What does it mean to be "born again"? How does it happen?

According to John 3:16-17, for what purpose *did/didn't* God send the *Loving Christ* into the world? How does that affect the way you look at Christ?

Day Twenty-Seven:
The Accepting Christ

Scripture Reading: John 4:1-42

Prayer

Father,

Your Son's ministry consisted of divine appointments. No meeting was an accident, no conversation a coincidence, and no "hello" a happenstance. His day was deliberate, his interactions intentional—every step of his foot had the imprint of divine necessity. Therefore, it was no mistake that he approached, acquainted himself with, and accepted the "unacceptables" of society.

He had grace *full* conversations with grace *less* individuals. He mixed with the "mixed bloods": the Samaritans. He touched the "untouchables": the lepers. He picked up and pieced together the shambles of a broken woman's life—five times she was a marital failure and now she was living with a man who could represent the sixth. But your Son didn't sweep her away with judgment; rather he swept her up into the kingdom of God. He didn't overlook the ugliness of the sin but he did look through it and past it to the beauty of the sinner. Approval? No. Acceptance? Yes!

During this day, I want to experience the divine appointments of the *Accepting Christ*. Help me see the divine imprint of his footsteps on every pebble of my path, the touch of his hand on the hours of my day, and the sweep of his love over all the broken areas of my life. Remind me that approval is based on works but acceptance is by grace. Amen

Meditation

She's a Samaritan; he's a Jew. Woman. Man. Her life is a mess and he is the Messiah. He is Life itself. Culturally she's not allowed to mix with him, socially she's not allowed to be seen with him, and spiritually she's not allowed to talk to him. She's prohibited from being anywhere near him. It is he, therefore, not she, who arranges a meeting.

As he leaves Judea, he leaves with a sense of divine necessity. He must go through Samaria, he must go to the town of Sychar to sit at Jacob's well, and he must see her. He predestines the events of the encounter. He premeditates the appointed time and place. He predetermines the subject, direction, and outcome of their conversation.

> *"Now he had to go through Samaria. So he came to a town in Samaria called Sychar, near the plot of ground Jacob had given to his son Joseph. Jacob's well was there, and Jesus, tired as he was from the journey, sat down by the well. It was about the sixth hour.*
>
> *When a Samaritan woman came to draw water, Jesus said to her, 'Will you give me a drink?' "* [1]

She comes at the sixth hour. It's the noon hour, the hottest part of the day, the time when everyone else is resting inside. As she carries her water jar, she tries to position it in such a way as to veil her eyes from the glare of the sun. Noon may be the hottest part of the day, but for her, it's emotionally the most refreshing. The sixth hour is an oasis because, at noon, she's alone.

When she comes at noon, she's exposed only to the sun. At the sixth hour, there is no blistering gossip from the local women, no searing stares, no scorching judgment, no exposure of her sins, no disclosure of personal indiscretions. At noon, the mistakes of her past and the problems in her present can stay eclipsed, covered, and blurred in the shadows of loneliness.

But at noon he's there. Jesus is sitting alone up against her well. He asks her for a drink. But he's a Jew and she's a Samaritan, and pure bloods and mixed bloods don't mix. Instead, they defile, detest, and despise each other.

> *"The Samaritan woman said to him, 'You are a Jew and I am a Samaritan woman. How can you ask me for a drink?' (For Jews do not associate with Samaritans.)*
>
> *Jesus answered her, 'If you knew the gift of God and who it is that asks you for a drink, you would have asked him and he would have given you living water.' "* [2]

He's thirsty and she has water. But that's just the trickle that starts the stream of dialogue. The real flow of the conversation is that she's dying of thirst and he has living water. Her soul is barren, her spirit of worship is parched, her attitude is arid, and her relationships with men are like dust in the wind: here with her today, blown away tomorrow.

> *" 'I have no husband,' she replied. Jesus said to her, 'You are right when you say you have no husband. The fact is, you have had five husbands, and the man you now have is not your husband. What you have just said is quite true.' "* [3]

She tries to divert this deluge of intimate facts with a theological question. She asks him about the proper place of worship, "Is it my mountain, Mt. Gerizim, or your mountain, Jerusalem?" [4]

He breaks the dam open by saying,

"Neither! It's not about a place; it's about a Person. It's not about sanctuary and Torah; it's about spirit and truth. It's about worshiping the one you know and knowing the one you worship."

Swept away by his words, she responds,

" 'I know that Messiah' (called Christ) 'is coming. When he comes, he will explain everything to us.'

Then Jesus declared, 'I who speak to you am he.' " [5]

Living Water floods her life with grace, overwhelms her with love, and overflows her with hope. Her old life has been drowned. Its shame has been swept away. A new life has blossomed out of the wilderness.

The *Accepting Christ* doesn't accept her behavior but he accepts her. He sits at the well alone, at noon. He had made an appointment. Jew was going to meet Samaritan, Messiah was going to meet with a woman whose life was a mess, and living water was going to meet wilderness.

The two met and she got wet.

[1]John 4:4-7 [2]John 4:9-10 [3]John 4:17-18 [4]John 4:20 [5]John 4:25-26

Reflection

What's the thirst that the *Accepting Christ* wants to quench in your life?

How has the *Accepting Christ* gone out of his way to meet you? What well does Jesus sit at as he waits for you?

What's the difference between approval and acceptance? How does Jesus accept you without approving of your actions?

What would you do if someone told you everything you ever did? (John 4:27-42)

Day Twenty-Eight:
The Grieving Christ

Scripture Reading: John 11:1-44

Prayer

Father,

As your Son came to the tomb of Lazarus, "the one that he loved", he was ambushed by his emotions. Two intense feelings—love and loss—rushed at him from opposite directions. They surprised, seized, and disarmed him. He was overwhelmed by the height of his love for his friend but overcome by the depth of the loss. Without warning, love had seized his heart; without mercy, loss had a devil's grip on his gut. Doubled over, he fell to his knees, crossed his arms over his stomach, buried his head, rocked up and down, and began to grieve.

More than grief, the tears were a testimony of his love. More than weeping, this was witness. More than a solemn moment by a grave, this was something sacred. His grieving was an outward sign of an inner, sacred tearing of his heart. He just wasn't crying; his heart was bleeding.

During this day, I want to know that the *Grieving Christ* is deeply moved by me. Help me believe that he calls me, knows me, and refers to me as, "the one that I love". Show me not only that he loves me, but that he also weeps over any death in my life. I pray this in the name of the one who grieves death but also raises the dead. Amen.

Meditation

Two sisters, their brother, and Jesus. They aren't just friends; they're family. They might not be connected by genetics or related by blood but they are bound together by love. And so when the brother, Lazarus, gets sick, the sisters send word to Jesus, "Lord, the one you love is sick." [1]

Underneath the news, unspoken but understood, is an urgent plea, "Come quickly!" But Jesus deliberately delays.

> *"When he heard this, Jesus said, 'This sickness will not end in death. No, it is for God's glory so that God's Son may be glorified through it.' Jesus loved Martha and her sister and Lazarus. Yet when he heard that Lazarus was sick, he stayed where he was two more days."* [2]

The "one that he loves" is sick and he deliberately delays. It's two more days before he goes to Bethany. What type of love is this? What type of friend? What type of Messiah? For Jesus, the outcome is certain—Lazarus' sickness will not end in death. Death may be a stop along the way, but it's not the last stop on the journey. It's the next to the last stop. Resurrection is the final destination.

His love for Lazarus is certain. Though Jesus is absent, his love isn't diluted, his bond of friendship isn't weakened, and his affection doesn't wane. Though he's late, he still loves. Jesus is certain that he will be glorified through the sickness, the sorrow, and the suffering of the next few days. In the valley of death, he will be exalted.

But what's certain for Jesus is not so certain for Mary and Martha. They had sent word for him to come. They were certain that he would stop his activity, make

Lazarus a priority, and rush to Bethany. And so they look down the road. They wait. They wonder where he is. But while they wait and because Jesus delays, their brother dies.

When Jesus finally does come, there's an emotional distance. A gap of uncertainty has been created by their grief.

"Does he still love us?"
"If he does care about us, why didn't he come?"
"Why is he so late?"

The loss of Lazarus has created a degree of separation between Jesus and the sisters. Mary, the more emotionally tender of the two, chooses to stay at home when Jesus enters Bethany. Martha, the more assertive and verbal, marches out.

"When Martha heard that Jesus was coming, she went out to meet him, but Mary stayed at home.

'Lord,' Martha said to Jesus, 'if you had been here, my brother would not have died. But I know that even now God will give you whatever you ask.'

Jesus said to her, 'Your brother will rise again.' " 3

Eventually, Mary comes and weeps at his feet.

Both sisters begin with the same premise, "If you would have been here ...". Martha punctuates her case with firm, direct words, spoken straight to his face. Mary weeps her conclusion as she wets his feet with her tears.

The source of the heartache is that the sisters know that everything could have been different. It didn't have to end this way. While Jesus could have done something, he didn't. Not yet.

"When Jesus saw her weeping, and the Jews who had come along with her also weeping, he was deeply moved in spirit and troubled. 'Where have you laid him?' he asked.

'Come and see, Lord,' they replied.

Jesus wept.

Then the Jews said, 'See how he loved him!' " [4]

As he approaches the tomb of Lazarus, Jesus is overwhelmed with emotion. Suddenly, out of nowhere, his love for his friend and the loss of his friend meet, mingle, and then ignite in his gut. He doubles over, falls to the ground, and begins to mourn.

This is a sacred moment—holy ground. Nothing is said and yet everything is said. His emotions speak without him saying a word. His weeping is a witness and his tears a testimony. The grieving isn't planned, orchestrated, choreographed, or done on cue. Such contrivance would profane the purity of his pain. Love and loss have ambushed him. Mourning comes no other way. Those around Jesus can only acknowledge, "See how he loved him!"

But the day doesn't end with mourning; mourning is only a place to stop on the way to rejoicing. Jesus goes to the tomb, orders the stone to be taken away, and then shouts to his friend, "Lazarus, come out!"[5] The dead man comes walking. In the resurrection of Lazarus, Jesus reveals his glory. In the death of his friend, the *Grieving Christ* shows his heart. Which is the greater miracle, a dead man walking or the Messiah weeping?

[1]John 11:3 [2]John 11:4-6 [3]John 11:20-23 [4]John 11:33-36 [5]John 11:43

Reflection

Do you remember the last time you wept?
What did the weeping reveal?

Have you ever said, "Lord, if you would have been here ...""?
If so, what were the circumstances?

What comfort does it bring to you to know that Jesus
wept?

What death are you grieving?
What resurrection are you celebrating?

Sabbath Day of Reflection

"On my bed I remember you;
I think of you through the watches of the night.

Because you are my help, I sing in
the shadow of your wings."

Psalm 63:6-7

A Sabbath day of reflection entails both a look into the mirror of our humanity and a stare into the majesty of his divinity.

One shows us ourselves.
The other shows us Christ

The mirror reflects sin.
His majesty reflects grace.

The mirror shows us what we have done.
Majesty shows what he is about to do.

Reflection

As you lay on your bed through the watches of the night, what thoughts of Christ come to mind?

What do you see as you look into the mirror? What reflection stares back at you?

What do you see as you look into his majesty? What do you think he is about to do during the next leg of your journey?

Day Twenty-Nine:
The Promising Christ

Scripture Reading: John 13:31–14:31

Prayer

Father,

The closer your Son moved toward the cross, the more intimate his conversation with his disciples became. His final words weren't flippant, trite, or wanting. Everything he said was measured, meaningful, and meant to memorialize his love. Every word was punctuated with a promise: his presence, a place with many rooms, and the coming of the Counselor. This Counselor was the one who would represent, teach, and remind the disciples about your Son.

During this day, when my heart is troubled, may the *Promising Christ* give me his peace. I need the peace that surpasses human understanding: a peace that is beyond this world, apart from human striving, and which rests solely in the promises of your Son, Jesus the Christ. It's in his name I pray. Amen

Meditation

On the eve of his betrayal, Jesus knew that everything was about to change.

In a matter of hours, one disciple—Judas—would betray him. Another—Peter—would deny him. All the others would scatter, flee, and disown him. Soon, the only words he would hear would be those of accusing officials, denouncing religious leaders, scoffing crowds, mocking soldiers, and insulting robbers. His family wouldn't speak. His disciples would hold their tongues. Even his Father would remain silent.

And so on the last evening that he is with his disciples—the ones that he loved and who loved him—there is urgency in every sentence he speaks. There is significance in every syllable and insistence in every intonation. He needs to speak to them and they need to hear what he has to say because all of their hearts are troubled.

> *"My children, I will be with you only a little longer. You will look for me, and just as I told the Jews, so I tell you now: Where I am going, you cannot come...*
>
> *Do not let your hearts be troubled. Trust in God; trust also in me. In my Father's house are many rooms; if it were not so, I would have told you. I am going there to prepare a place for you. And if I go and prepare a place for you, I will come back and take you to be with me that you also may be where I am. You know the way to the place where I am going."* [1]

In a few days, their worlds are going to be different. His disciples will know only promise. Jesus will revel in fulfillment. They will live in reality; he will dwell in eternity. They will be fighting off the gates of hell while he will have gone through hell and passed through the gates of heaven.

Though their worlds are going to be different, Jesus promises that he will always be with them, but in a different way. He might be physically absent from their sight but he'll be invisibly present. They won't be able to see him, touch him, or walk and talk with him like they once did. Yet he'll still be there. He's not going to leave them behind; he's just going on ahead.

"I will not leave you as orphans; I will come to you." 2

He's not going to leave them alone. He won't leave them unprotected, without support, as orphans. He's going on ahead because, as the carpenter's son, he has something to build.

As long as the disciples live on the earth, their lives and their homes will only be those of promise: dwellings of the now and the not yet, abodes of anticipation. But Jesus assures his disciples that, after he rises from the dead, he will be busy building, preparing, and constructing homes of heavenly fulfillment for them.

But between the promise and the fulfillment, the dreaming and the coming true, the blueprints and the housewarming, is a construction period—a time of the troubled heart.

In the *in between years,* the heart yearns, longs, and wonders when real life—eternal life—will begin. In the *in between years,* the spirit dreams, hopes, and prays for wholeness. Those in the *in between years* know that there is something more, something unfinished, and something yet to be. Between the promise and the fulfillment are the years when the heart is troubled. The longer the heart waits, the wearier it becomes.

As the heart grows weary, the memory of the promise and the Person who gave it tends to fade. And so, before he goes to the cross, Jesus promises his disciples a comforter, the Counselor.

> *"All this I have spoken while still with you. But the Counselor, the Holy Spirit, whom the Father will send in my name, will teach you all things and will remind you of everything I have said to you. Peace I leave with you; my peace I give you. I do not give to you as the world gives. Do not let your hearts be troubled and do not be afraid."* [3]

On the eve of Jesus' betrayal, every word is punctuated with a promise. He promises his presence. He promises the Counselor. He promises a heavenly home.

The promises are the eternal blueprints. They're the two-dimensional renderings of a multi-dimensional reality. They only foreshadow what the house is going to look like.

Fulfillment is the finished product. It's the day the *Promising Christ* ...

Pounds the last nail,
Finishes the final coat of paint,
Puts the name on the mailbox.

And then he comes to his own,
takes them to his Father's house and says,
"Let's go home!"

[1]John 13:33; 14:1-4 [2]John 14:18 [3]John 14:25-27

Reflection

Into what area of your life do you need the *Promising Christ* to say, "Do not let your hearts be troubled"?

What comfort is there in knowing that the carpenter's son is preparing a place for you?

What promises of Christ bring you peace—peace unlike the world could ever give?

How has the Counselor—the Holy Spirit—taught you all things and reminded you of the promises and presence of Christ?

Day Thirty:
The Commanding Christ

Scripture Reading: John 15:1-27

Prayer

Father,

In the final hours of your Son's life, when time was short and words needed to be few, he gathered his disciples around him. In a solemn and yet soothing way he promised them his presence, he prayed for their protection, and he commanded them to love one another. At the root of his command, there was a living example, not a heavy-handed mandate:

"Love each other as I have loved you." [1]

Your Son knew that forced love was no love. It must happen spontaneously, internally not externally. It must grow, blossom, and then bear fruit.

As he laid the seed of his soul into the soil of their hearts, he spoke of a vine, branches, and fruit—living metaphors for his love. He wanted them to remain in his love as well as live out of it. With him, relationship was the key.

During this day, I want to be connected to the *Commanding Christ*. I want to live in his love and love out of his example. I want to bear much fruit, fruit that will last. Help me understand that the seed of love is sacrifice, the root of sacrifice is death, and the fruit of death is new life. It's in his name I pray. Amen.

Meditation

As Jesus moves closer to his death, he moves closer to his disciples. The final moments that he shares with them are sacred treasures. He wants to bury these treasures deep into their hearts, safe from thieves, secure from robbers, and protected from the approaching pirate of death.

He sees their troubled hearts and promises them his presence, a place in heaven, and a peace unlike the world could ever give.

Nothing is held back.

He senses their grief and so he weeps with them, lays bare his heart, and pours out his love.

Nothing is hidden.

He knows their fear of the future and prays for their protection.

"Please, Father. Nothing harmful."

His final words form a string of pearls, forever cherished and worn around the necks of his disciples. His final "I love you!" is a ring of promise for their collective finger, a reminder that he is going to prepare a bridal suite and will one day reappear to sweep them off their feet. His final prayers create a crown of jewels: not only a protective covering for their head but also a reminder that they are royalty. His last breath is a ransom for many. Debt paid in full!

As he prepares for his death, he cherishes the final hours with them. Nothing else matters or exists. In one evening, he lives a lifetime of love. He leaves nothing unsaid, nothing undone, nothing unclear.

On this final night, all he wants is love.
   He wants relationship.
      He wants intimacy—he in them and they in
      him.

But the intimacy that Jesus desires speaks another language. Simple words fail to capture the depth, the color, and the texture of his longing and so he exchanges the black and white order of words for the palette and array of a word picture. He paints a metaphor of intimacy—a vine, branches, and fruit.

> *"Remain in me, and I will remain in you. No branch can bear fruit by itself; it must remain in the vine. Neither can you bear fruit unless you remain in me.*
>
> *I am the vine; you are the branches. If a man remains in me and I in him, he will bear much fruit; apart from me you can do nothing."* [2]

He's the vine and they are the branches. They are joined, connected, and grafted into him by love. He loves them and they are to live in that love as well as love out of it. They are to bear fruit: much fruit, fruit that will last.

But the fruit at the end of the vine is only a by-product, a sign, and a result of the relationship. If there's no fruit, then there's no relationship. If bad fruit results, then the branch is attached to the wrong vine. But if there's much fruit—fruit that will last—then there is intimacy. And these seeds sown in intimacy are to produce a harvest of love.

*"As the Father has loved me, so have I loved you.
Now remain in my love. If you obey my commands,
you will remain in my love, just as I have obeyed
my Father's commands and remain in his love. I
have told you this so that my joy may be in you
and that your joy may be complete. My command
is this: Love each other as I have loved you. Greater
love has no one than this, that he lay down his life
for his friends."* [3]

With the image of intimacy painted, Jesus leaves the
colorful metaphor of the vineyard. He speaks plainly: no
figures to figure out, no layered meanings. He simply
says,

"Love each other as I have loved you." [4]

It's a command, but it's a command flowing from the
authority of example and not the threat of punishment.
He doesn't shout,

"Just love!"
        "Do it!"
                "I command it."

For the *Commanding Christ,* forced love is no love.
Rather he whispers,

"Just as I have loved you, you also love."

Love is a response,
        a result,
                and the fruit
of an intimate relationship with him.

[1]John 15:12 [2]John 15:4-5 [3]John 15:9-13 [4]John 15:12

Reflection

What's the greatest act of love that anyone has shown you?

What does intimacy with Christ look like? How does it happen?

How does the *Commanding Christ* prompt you to love?

What does it mean to live in the love of the
Commanding Christ as well as live out of his example?

Day Thirty-One:
The Anointed Christ

Scripture Reading: Mark 14:1-11

Prayer

Father,

Your Son was called the Christ, the Messiah—which means "the Anointed One". You chose him to be the alabaster jar of heaven—a precious vial that you broke open, poured out, and lavished on humanity. His life carried with it the fragrance of grace, his death the aroma of forgiveness, and his resurrection the redolence of redemption. This "Alabaster Jar of Heaven" was price-less, his scent eternal, and the love in his bouquet undeserved. In your Son, you poured out divine extravagance.

During this day, in response to the extravagant love of Christ, I want be like Mary. In some intimate way, I want to come, break open my alabaster jar of expensive per-fume, and anoint the body of Christ. Though my actions may be misunderstood by the world, though they may be described as "a waste", and though those around me may rebuke me harshly, I still want my love to be extravagant. I want to hear the words that the *Anointed Christ* spoke to Mary spoken of me:

> *"She did what she could. She didn't hold anything back. And what she did for me was a beautiful thing."*

It's in his name I pray. Amen.

Meditation

The foul odor of foul play is in the air and the stench is coming from the chief priests and teachers of the law. They're saturated with anger. They reek of hypocrisy, deceit, and decaying spirituality. They're salivating at the thought of Jesus' death. All they're waiting for is the right moment, a moment without incident or riots. After all, no one wants to start a big stink during Passover.

> *"Now the Passover and the Feast of Unleavened Bread were only two days away, and the chief priests and the teachers of the law were looking for some sly way to arrest Jesus and kill him. 'But not during the Feast,' they said, 'or the people may riot.' "* 1

Into this stench comes a waft of fresh air. This light breeze is Mary, the sister of Lazarus, the brother who had been raised from the dead. Her presence, tender emotion, and the purity of her devotion swirl around him and fill the room like a sweet perfume. Her love brings the bouquet of life to a man who smells the scent of death.

Accompanying her love is a sacred sign and token. She brings an alabaster jar of pure nard. It's expensive, more than a year's wages worth. It's extraordinary, far beyond something that is commonplace. It's extravagant, surpassing rational sensibility or fiscal responsibility.

She brings the alabaster jar, breaks the neck, and pours it over his head. It's not the reasonable thing to do, or the most rational. But it is the right thing. She's not out of her mind; she's acting out of her heart.

*"While he was in Bethany, reclining at the table
in the home of a man known as Simon the Leper,
a woman came with an alabaster jar of very
expensive perfume, made of pure nard. She broke
the jar and poured the perfume on his head.*

*Some of those present were saying indignantly to
one another, 'Why this waste of perfume? It could
have been sold for more than a year's wages and
the money given to the poor.' And they rebuked her
harshly."* [2]

Her extravagance brings a harsh rebuke. The disciples,
specifically Judas—the keeper of the moneybag and a
thief—shame her.[3] All they see is an economic transac-
tion. They don't see the currency of love that is being
exchanged. All they look at is the bottom line of the
budget and ask, "Why this waste of perfume?"

They've done a cost benefit analysis and they've con-
cluded that this expenditure is a bad investment. In their
eyes, it will pay no returns, no earthly dividends, and
there will be no interest. They call her act of extravagance "a waste", "bad stewardship", and "excessive". Jesus,
the recipient of her love and the sole source of her investment, hears all of these harsh rebukes and wonders,

*"If they rebuke her, aren't they rebuking me? If her
act of love is 'a waste' than am I, the one she loves,
'a waste'? Am I worth her extravagance or are there
other things—better things—that the money could
have been spent on? Am I a good investment?"*

Jesus answers their rebukes with a rebuke of his own.
He stands against the disciples, stands by Mary's side,
and stands up for himself. He explains the economy of
her actions.

" 'Leave her alone,' said Jesus. 'Why are you bothering her? She has done a beautiful thing to me. The poor you will always have with you, and you can help them any time you want. But you will not always have me. She did what she could. She poured perfume on my body beforehand to prepare for my burial. I tell you the truth, wherever the gospel is preached throughout the world, what she has done will also be told, in memory of her.' " [4]

The *Anointed Christ* gets up, shields Mary, and then stands with his arm around her. His pores are saturated, his clothes are covered, and his hair is still dripping with the extravagant perfume that came from the alabaster jar now broken on the floor. He looks into Mary's eyes, breathes deep, closes his eyes, smiles, and savors the aroma of her love.

He then turns to his disciples and says,

"She has done a beautiful thing for me. She did what she could. She poured perfume on my body beforehand to prepare it for my burial." [5]

Mary had just invested everything she had. She didn't keep anything back, hidden away, saved for another day. While Jesus was in Bethany, she wanted to live with lavish love. And it was that fragrance of lavish love that sustained him on the cross. Even the stench of death couldn't overpower the aroma of her love. With every labored breath, he closed his eyes and savored the scent of the perfume.

As he did, he remembered her.

[1]Mark 14:1-2 [2]Mark 14:3-5 [3]John 12:4-5 [4]Mark 14:6-9 [5]Mark 14:6,8

Reflection

Have you ever been rebuked harshly for an act of love that you did for Christ? What was the action? What was the rebuke?

Mary did what she could. What beautiful thing could you do to anoint Christ? What act of extravagance would express your devotion?

Mary was remembered as the one who anointed Christ. How will the world remember your love for Jesus? What memorial will you leave?

How has the fragrance of Christ's life, death, and resurrection scented your life?

Day Thirty-Two:
The Serving Christ

Scripture Reading: John 13:1-38

Prayer

Father,

Your Son was the Messiah who got his hands dirty.

Though his disciples called him "Master", he took the posture of a servant. Though he was the greatest among them, he became the least. Though he was the Prince of Heaven, he took off his royal robes, picked up the basin and the towel, bent the knee, and washed his disciples' feet.

He served even though he knew that in a few hours one of them would betray him, another would deny him, and all would scatter and abandon him. He humbled himself, descended into greatness, and showed them the full measure of his love.

During this day, I want to follow the example of the *Serving Christ*. Don't let me passively sit, look around at others, and wait to be served. Instead, as I walk through this day, prompt me to serve, to humble myself, and to get my hands dirty with the ministry of the Messiah— washing dirty feet.

It's in his name I pray. Amen.

Meditation

Century after century, year after year, and month after month, the pages of the redemptive calendar have been turning. But now the long awaited day is almost here. The clock of Jesus' crucifixion is about to strike fulfillment, the bell of his death is about to toll, and the trumpet of his resurrection is about to blow.

His time has come.

The Father's eternal plans have an earthly timetable - Friday. On that day, the one who had jumped into time will be nailed to a cross, die, and on the third day he will rise and jump back into eternity.

> *"It was just before the Passover Feast. Jesus knew that the time had come for him to leave this world and go to the Father. Having loved his own who were in the world, he now showed them the full extent of his love."* [1]

It was the Feast of Passover: a time to remember the blood of the lamb on the doorposts, the great deliverance from the angel of death, and the exodus out of bondage. For centuries, this feast was observed. But it was a feast that always left one hungry for more, craving ultimate deliverance, and starving for a spiritual exodus from the bondage of sin.

During this Passover Feast, the longing will be fulfilled. The Good Shepherd will become the sacrificial lamb. In a few hours, the blood of the Lamb of God will be on the wood of the cross, the angel of death will pass over the sins of humanity, and there will be deliverance. Ultimate exodus.

But before the Feast of Passover is fulfilled, Jesus, the Lamb of God, wants to show his disciples the full measure of his love. The one who is about to sit on the throne of heaven bends his knee, takes off his royal robes, and serves.

> *"The evening meal was being served, and the devil had already prompted Judas Iscariot, son of Simon, to betray Jesus. Jesus knew that the Father had put all things under his power, and that he had come from God and was returning to God; so he got up from the meal, took off his outer clothing, and wrapped a towel around his waist. After that, he poured water into a basin and began to wash his disciples' feet, drying them with the towel that was wrapped around him."* [2]

It's one thing to love someone when you know everything that he's done. It's another thing to love him when you know everything he's about to do.

The devil has just put a dagger of betrayal in the hand of Judas. In a few hours, he'll arrange a time, a place, and a signal for the chief priests:

> late at night,
>   in the Garden of Gethsemane,
>   with a kiss.

With clean feet but a soiled heart, Judas will approach Jesus with a smile, draw close, kiss his cheek, stab, and then give the dagger a twist. Jesus sees the betrayer's dagger and yet he still exposes his heart. He takes the basin, washes the feet of Judas, and dries them with the towel. It's as if he's saying to him,

> *"I know what you're about to do. But before you do it, I want you to know that I love you."*

There's another dagger in the room—the dagger of denial. Before the evening is over and before the rooster crows, Peter will deny Jesus three times. When questioned about his association with Jesus, he will curse and swear like the salty fisherman that he is. Not once, or twice, but three times he will say, "I don't know him!" After this night of curses, his whole body—not just his feet—will need to be cleansed. Though Jesus sees the dagger of denial, he exposes his heart. He washes Peter's feet. He serves. In the cool of the water and with the caress of the towel, Jesus says,

> *"Peter, I know what you're about to do. But before you do it, I want you to know that, though you deny me, I'll never deny you."*

The *Serving Christ* is the Prince who is among paupers, the Master who is among servants, and the greatest among the least. He's the one who takes off his royal robes, humbles himself, picks up the basin and the towel, bends the knee, descends into greatness, and shows his disciples—all of them, even Judas and Peter—the full measure of his love. The Purity of Heaven gets his hands dirty, washes their feet, and then invites them to do the same for one another.

> *"Now that I, your Lord and Teacher, have washed your feet, you also should wash one another's feet. I have set you an example that you should do as I have done for you. I tell you the truth, no servant is greater than his master, nor is a messenger greater than the one who sent him."* [3]

The filth of denial says, "I don't know you."
The mud of betrayal says, "I don't want you."
Even so, the *Serving Christ* still washes feet.

[1]John 13:1 [2]John 13:2-5 [3]John 13:14-16

Reflection

What does it feel like to be served? Has anyone ever "washed your feet"? If so, how did it feel?

It's one thing to serve your friends; it's another to serve those who betray and deny you. In what way(s) can you serve both your friends as well as those who have or will hurt you?

Why is it so unnatural to "pick up the basin and towel" and "wash one another's feet"?

Even though the *Serving Christ* knew what Judas and Peter were about to do, he washed their feet. How does that comfort you?

Day Thirty-Three:
The Interceding Christ

Scripture Reading: John 17:1-26

Prayer

Father,

Throughout your Son's ministry, he invaded the realm and destroyed the work of the evil one. He healed the sick. He cast out demons. He raised the dead. He interfered with the Devil's plans. He intervened in divine and providential ways. He got involved, jumped into the fray of humanity, and put himself in between the hate of the Destroyer and the beloved children of heaven.

As the time for him to visibly leave his disciples approached, he prayed his last earthly prayer. As he prayed, he stood between heaven and earth, lifted his head, extended his hands, and placed the ones that he loved into your arms. His last prayer began on earth but he promised that it would continue throughout eternity.

During this day, give me faith to believe that the *Interceding Christ* lifts his head toward heaven for me. Help me know that, as he prays, he gets in between the destructive plans of the evil one and the purposes that you have for my life. Help me realize that he is an eternal "go between", an intercessor, the one who sits at your right hand and speaks to you on my behalf. As he prays for me, I pray all of this in his name. Amen.

Meditation

Prayer lifts the head toward heaven. When one prays upward, when the head is lifted, the eyes can't look around at the many worries that the world brings. They can't look down in depression or close in despair. When one prays, the head lifts; the heart opens; and the eyes see the open arms of the Father.

In this moment, Jesus needs to see the Father.

It's the final hours of his life. As his eyes look ahead, he sees betrayal and denial. He recognizes mock trials, but real condemnation. He sees rejection, pain, and suffering. He winces as he sees his crucifixion, death, and burial.

He looks up.

> *"After Jesus said this, he looked toward heaven and prayed:*
>
>> *'Father, the time has come. Glorify your Son, that your Son may glorify you. For you granted him authority over all people that he might give eternal life to all those you have given him. Now this is eternal life: that they may know you, the only true God, and Jesus Christ, whom you have sent. I have brought you glory on earth by completing the work you gave me to do. And now, Father, glorify me in your presence with the glory I had with you before the world began.' "* [1]

Everything is right in this prayer.

Jesus is in a right relationship with the one who sent him. He begins his prayer tenderly, affectionately, and relationally. He calls out, "Father". He is the right person, who is in the right place, at the right time, and so he affirms, "the time has come". It's the right redemptive moment. The eternal purpose of his Father's hands has met the hands of earthly time and so he petitions, "Glorify your Son, that your Son may glorify you."

As Jesus lifts his head, peace invades his pain. Its soothing voice whispers,

"Everything is going to be all right."

After Jesus prays for himself, he begins to pray for his disciples. All of those who have believed in him are gifts from his Father. As he prepares to visibly leave the ones he loves, he intercedes. He pleads. He acts as a go between. He extends his hands toward heaven and gently places the ones he loves back into the arms of his Father.

> *"I have revealed you to those whom you gave me out of the world. They were yours; you gave them to me and they have obeyed your word ...*
>
> *I will remain in the world no longer, but they are still in the world, and I am coming to you. Holy Father, protect them by the power of your name— the name you gave me—so that they may be one as we are one ...*
>
> *My prayer is not that you take them out of the world but that you protect them from the evil one."* 2

As he prays, his heart beats fast. He knows that the world he entered is not the paradise he once helped create. It's a shattered place. It's far from the image of perfection he had painted. It's a deceptive place; absolute truth is distorted or denied, heavenly reality is blurred, and the longing for eternity is being eclipsed by the perversion of earthly pleasure. It's a satanic place: the devil's playground. It was the evil one who had invaded the Garden. Sin followed. Paradise was lost. Death, destruction, and decay took up residence.

The world isn't a safe place and yet he doesn't ask his Father to take the ones that he loves out of the world. Rather, he prays for their protection. Protect them?

> Why not retreat?
>> Why not leave?
>>> Why not escape?

The *Interceding Christ* doesn't know how to retreat; he only knows how to invade. In the womb of a virgin, he invades his dying world in order that it might be born again. Through his miracles, he invades and destroys the work of the evil one. In his death and resurrection, he invades the realm of hell, takes the keys of sin and death, and declares victory. And as he invades his world, he asks the ones he loves to follow him,

"Invade the world with me!"

That's why he prays,

"Protect them!"

It's his last prayer on earth but it's a prayer that he will continue to pray throughout eternity. Except in eternity, he won't have to look up to see his Father's face; he'll be able to look straight into his eyes.

"Christ Jesus, who died—more than that, who was raised to life—is at the right hand of God and is also interceding for us." [3]

[1]John 17:1-5 [2]John 17:6,11,15 [3]Romans 8:34

Reflection

What causes your eyes to look around in worry, down in depression, or close in despair?

How does prayer lift your head toward heaven? How does it change the way you view your life?

From what do you need protection?

What comfort is there in knowing that the *Interceding Christ* is praying for you—that he has extended his hands and placed you in the hands of the Father?

Day Thirty-Four:
The Triumphant Christ

Scripture Reading: Matthew 21:1-11

Prayer

Father,

As your Son entered Jerusalem, the crowds shouted, "Hosanna!" Behind, before, and all around, they welcomed him as the long awaited Messianic King. They declared him to be the Son of David and they paved the royal highway with their garments, palm branches, and psalms of praise. The flame of Messianic expectations burned hot; the swirling mass of people began to boil over with nationalistic hope.

However, as the days passed, the crowds' dream of an earthly king turned to vapor. Your Son was a king but not the type of king that they wanted. His kingdom was not of this world; he didn't come with armies, swords, or political agendas; his enemies were not the legions of Rome but the spiritual forces of evil in the heavenly realms; he came riding on a colt, meek and gentle. He was a Servant King. His eternal purpose didn't match their political expectations and so his coronation procession led not to a crown, a robe, or a throne—but to thorns, nakedness, and a triumphant cross.

During this day, help me welcome the *Triumphant Christ*. And as my Servant King walks through this day, help me run behind, before, and around him. Show me how to place my garments on the road, wave the palm branches, shout psalms of praise, and crown him Lord of all. It's in his name I pray. Amen.

Meditation

No two issues are more volatile than politics and religion.

On the day Jesus rides into Jerusalem, the hammer of nationalism hits the flint of messianic expectation and sparks begin to fly. Ever since the glory days of King David and the golden days of King Solomon, the people of Israel have longed for the Messianic King, the Son of David. They have outlived the Exile; they have outlasted the rule and reign of the Persians; they have outstayed the Hellenization of Alexander the Great; and they have survived the desecration of their temple by Antiochus Epiphanes. Now, as they wait for their Messianic King, they're riding out the iron rule of Rome.

In Jesus, the dream of the Messianic kingdom is rekindled. With every word, story, and teaching, a weathered stick is gathered; with every healing, a log is added; with every miracle, a match is struck. As he enters the Holy City, the Messianic bonfire is ready to blaze. His triumphant entry ignites a raging fire. It's stoked by national pride and fueled by dreams of a political theocracy. Hope has mixed all of the messianic ingredients together. The cauldron of a king is stirred. It's beginning to boil and kingdom expectations are overflowing.

> *"As they approached Jerusalem and came to Bethphage on the Mount of Olives, Jesus sent two disciples, saying to them, 'Go to the village ahead of you, and at once you will find a donkey tied there, with her colt by her. Untie them and bring them to me.'*
>
> *The disciples went and did as Jesus had instructed them. They brought the donkey and the colt, placed their cloaks on them, and Jesus sat on them. A very large crowd spread their cloaks on the road, while*

others cut branches from the trees and spread them on the road. The crowds that went ahead of him and those that followed shouted,

> *'Hosanna to the Son of David!'*
> *'Blessed is he who comes in the name of the Lord!'*
> *'Hosanna in the highest!' "* [1]

The crowds shout for his coronation. They crown him the Son of David. They lay their cloaks on the ground to pave the way for royalty, and as the palms wave, they shout psalms of praise. But in the days that follow his triumphant entry, their *experience* with Jesus fails to meet their *expectations* of him.

In less than a week, the people will become agitated; nationalistic hopes will seethe throughout Jerusalem and the dreams of a political, powerful, and physical nation of Israel will turn to vapor. When these things happen, only hate will boil over. Crowns will be switched—gold for thorns. Robes will be taken away. Coronation ceremonies will cease and crucifixion will commence.

Still, he is a king: just not the type of king they've been looking for. His kingdom is from another place—heaven, not earth. He rules with truth and grace, not threats and garrisons. He carries himself more like a servant than a sovereign. It is he who bends the knee and washes his disciples' feet. His throne is humility; his footstool is mercy. His rule is just but his reign flows out of love.

This king is different.

A colt confirmed what the prophet Zechariah had foretold.

> *"This took place to fulfill what was spoken through the prophet:*
>
> *'Say to the Daughter of Zion,*
> *See, your king comes to you,*
> *gentle and riding on a donkey,*
> *on a colt, the foal of a donkey.' "* [2]

His disciples should have known that Jesus was different. The crowds should have seen it. Here he is, entering Jerusalem riding sidesaddle on a colt: meek, mild, gentle, no threat to Rome. Still, he is royalty.

But their expectations blind and blur their eyes. The rule of their king, the scope of his kingdom, and their place in it have already been sketched, painted, and sealed in their minds. As with all earthly expectations, the picture on the canvas somehow became more beautiful and appealing than the model sitting on the stool.

Abstraction won out over reality.

The king in their dreams was much more attractive to them than the king in their real, wide-awake world. Still he comes. Royalty rides in on a beast of burden. The Messianic King takes up the basin and the towel of the servant. The sign of his coronation is not a golden throne or a jeweled crown but the wooden scepter of the cross. And as he holds the cross, he stands triumphant: robed in righteousness; crowned in glory; claiming and proclaiming authority.

[1]Matthew 21:1,2,6-9 [2]Matthew 21:4-5

Reflection

What does it feel like when your experience of God fails to meet your expectation of him?

What are your expectations of the King and his kingdom? What does it mean to live in the kingdom of God?

How can you place your garments on the royal road, wave the palm branches, shout psalms of praise, and crown him Lord of all?

Consider the following:

"When Jesus entered Jerusalem, the whole city was stirred and asked, 'Who is this Jesus?' " [1]

Has there ever been a time in your life when you were "stirred" and asked that question? If so, what was happening in your life?

[1]Matthew 21:10

Sabbath Day of Reception

"Ask and it will be given to you;
seek and you will find; knock and the door will be opened to
you. For everyone who asks receives; he who seeks finds; and
to him who knocks, the door will be opened."

Matthew 7:7-8

We live most of our lives with our hands closed. They wrap, grip, grasp, hold, clasp, clutch. Even in prayer, they fold. Fingers interlock and two hands become one closed fist.

On this Sabbath, God wants to open our hands to receive whatever he might want to give.

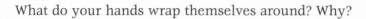

Reflection

What do your hands wrap themselves around? Why?

What are you asking for? What are you seeking? On what door are you knocking?

Before you continue your journey, open your hands. Turn your palms toward heaven and ask the Father to give you any and every gift he has for you.

Day Thirty-Five:
The Pleading Christ

Scripture Reading: Mark 14:12-42

Prayer

Father,

In the Garden, your Son, the Prince of Heaven, begged for a morsel of your mercy. Overwhelmed to the point of death, he extended his hands. With palms up, face down, and heart torn open, he appealed that the angel of death would pass over him. He asked that you would not only remove the cup of suffering but that you would pour it out somewhere else. But as your Son spoke, you remained silent. Your ears seemed to be deaf. Your lips didn't move. Your heart seemed as cold as the stone that he knelt against. Silence was your answer.

"No. There is no other way."

Somehow, your Son seemed to know that your devastating "no" was leading to a greater, divine "yes". You, Abba Father, as only you can do, were denying him something good in order that he might have the best.

As I beg for a morsel of your mercy, help me remember the *Pleading Christ*. Give me the strength to pray without having to hear your voice. Grant me the faith to understand that, though you're silent, you still hear. Grace me with the assurance that, though you say "no" to my good request, you're saving your "yes" for something better. Amen.

Meditation

It's a night of sacrifice and silence.

As the Feast of Unleavened Bread begins, the Passover lambs are chosen, led out, and killed. In an upper room, Jesus, the Passover Lamb, gathers with his disciples. In the bread and the wine, he breaks his body and pours out his blood—a new covenant of forgiveness for many.

On this night, Jesus isn't filled with sorrow; he's flooded with it. Distress has deluged his soul; fear has engulfed his future; and a torrent of troubles has swept away his hope. He's just before the point of death, still thrashing in the water, struggling for every breath.

But before he drowns in his despair, before he goes under for the last time, before the beginning of his end begins, he goes to the Garden to pray. As the sacrificial lambs bleat and bleed all throughout Jerusalem, the Lamb of God pleads with his Father. Like Isaac, the promised son of Abraham, he lies on the cold stone of the altar, bound by the cords of his Father's will, and wonders if there is some other way.

> *"They went to a place called Gethsemane, and Jesus said to his disciples, 'Sit here while I pray.' He took Peter, James and John along with him, and he began to be deeply distressed and troubled. 'My soul is overwhelmed with sorrow to the point of death,' he said to them. 'Stay here and keep watch.'*
>
> *Going a little farther, he fell to the ground and prayed that if possible the hour might pass from him. 'Abba, Father,' he said, 'everything is possible for you.*
>
> *Take this cup from me. Yet not what I will, but what you will.' "* [1]

When flooded with earthly sorrow, he fills the courts of heaven with a downpour of pleas. This deluge is mixed with drops of blood, sweat, and tears. He cries out to his Father to take away the cup of punishment. He begs him to remove this horrific hour from the clock. Like a child he persists, tugs, and appeals to his Father's heart. He asks him to make the impossible possible. He asks him to find some other way.

But as Jesus prays in the garden, the only responses that he receives are silence from his Father and snoring from his disciples. He had asked Peter, James, and John to stay awake, keep watch, and be alert so that they might not fall into temptation. He had pleaded with them to pray.

In this moment, he needs someone to intercede for him, to kneel beside him, to be next to him, and to suffer with him. He had done all of those things for his disciples and now he was asking them to do for him. He isn't looking for sympathy; right now he needs empathy. He doesn't want pity; he needs prayer. He needs them to enter in, participate in, and share in his agony.

He asks his disciples to support him. He begs them to stay awake, kneel beside him, and pray. But their eyes become heavy and they fall asleep. While he wrestles with a living nightmare, their bodies begin to relax, tension leaves, and they dream.

> *"Then he returned to his disciples and found them sleeping. 'Simon,' he said to Peter, 'are you asleep? Could you not keep watch for one hour? Watch and pray so that you will not fall into temptation. The spirit is willing, but the body is weak.'"* [2]

Returning to the place of prayer, he asks his Father again to spare him. He pleads with him to take away the cup: to pour out his judgment somewhere else or at least to consider quenching its thirst in some other way. But while the Son cries, the Father is silent. On this night, all of his pleas seem to go unanswered. By the silence, his Father speaks:

"No. There is no other way."

It's not the answer the *Pleading Christ* had hoped to hear. But his prayer was never a childish demand. He never shook his fist, stomped his feet, or flashed a sugary sweet, manipulative smile. He was simply a child crying out to his Abba, his Daddy, asking for something that he thought was good.

He knows the heart of his Father. If his Father says "no" to this plea, that means that he is about to give him something better. He knows his Father's heart. This devastating "no" has to be leading to a greater, divine "yes".

And it does!

In a few days, Jesus will be lying in a different garden, behind a different stone, with a different type of silence. But into that silence his Father will speak,

> "Yes!
> Live!
> Rise Again!"

[1]Mark 14:32-36 [2]Mark 14:37-38

Reflection

Do any of your prayers consist of blood, sweat, and tears? What is it like to pray those types of prayers?

What is it like to pray in deep agony and hear only silence from God?

What's it like for you to pray, "Yet not my will but your will be done."?

Has God's "no" ever led to a greater divine "yes" in your life?

Day Thirty-Six:
The Betrayed Christ

Scripture Reading: John 18:1-27

Prayer

Father,

On the eve of your Son's crucifixion, he stood alone. The adoring crowds, which had lined the road at his triumphant entry, had dissipated. When the detachment of soldiers came to the Garden with their torches, lanterns, and swords, no legions of heavenly angels had been dispatched. And when the wolf of Rome growled, bared his teeth, and bound the Shepherd, the little flock scattered. On that night, he was more than alone; he was abandoned. He was more than abandoned; he was disowned. He was more than disowned; he was betrayed. And these acts came not from the hands of strangers or the mouths of the nameless mass that had once followed him, but from his disciples: the ones he loved; his friends; those he called "family". One brother handed him over with a kiss. Another washed his hands of him and disowned him three times. On that night, your Son stood alone.

During this day, help me see all of the ways that I have abandoned, disowned, or betrayed my Brother, Jesus. And as my eyes are opened, help me understand why these acts are so painful. Help me realize that it's not the blow that comes from the hand of a stranger that hurts most but the betrayal that comes from the heart of a friend. And though I have abandoned Christ many times, assure me that he will never abandon, disown, or betray me. Amen.

Meditation

For Jesus, the Garden of Gethsemane is a familiar place. He and his disciples have gathered there many times. It's quiet, still, and intimate. It's also his favorite place: a place of peace and prayer, love and laughter, comfort and companionship. The Garden is one of those intimate places to which only the closest of friends are invited. But on this night, a familiar face leads an invasion of strangers into the secret place of Jesus' Gethsemane.

> *"Now Judas, who betrayed him, knew the place, because Jesus had often met there with his disciples. So Judas came to the grove, guiding a detachment of soldiers and some officials from the chief priests and Pharisees. They were carrying torches, lanterns and weapons."* [1]

A few hours earlier, Judas was part of Jesus' family. He sat next to his Messianic Brother at the Passover table. Together, they took the bread and dipped their hands into the bowl of fellowship. But now Judas is walking hand in hand with the enemy. He's the one in front carrying the torch. He's the one leading the way through the maze of the Garden. He's the one in front of the six hundred armed Roman soldiers. He's the one betraying Jesus for thirty pieces of silver.

Tonight, this betrayal isn't going to happen in foreign territory; it's going to happen on the family porch. It's not going to be a stab in the back; it's going to be intimate, face-to-face, with the pierce and then twist of a kiss. It's not going to be at the hand of a hidden assassin, but from the heart of a trusted friend.

Though Jesus knows all that is about to happen, he doesn't run, hide, or try to escape. He's aware that his hour has come and so he has resolved to live purposefully within the redemptive minutes that remain. He doesn't delay the timetable. He doesn't stall the salvation plan. He goes out and meets the mob. He finds his captors before they have a chance to find and capture him. He identifies himself before they identify him.

> *"Jesus, knowing all that was going to happen to him, went out and asked them, 'Who is it you want?'*
>
> *'Jesus of Nazareth,' they replied.*
>
> *'I am he,' Jesus said. (And Judas the traitor was standing there with them.) When Jesus said, 'I am he,' they drew back and fell to the ground."* [2]

And though he is able to drop a detachment of armed soldiers to the ground with a three-syllable phrase of identification, he still allows them to bind him and take him away. It's clear tonight that the one with the power is the one without the sword. But Peter doesn't see it that way.

> *"Then Simon Peter, who had a sword, drew it and struck the high priest's servant, cutting off his right ear. (The servant's name was Malchus.)*
>
> *Jesus commanded Peter, 'Put your sword away! Shall I not drink the cup the Father has given me?' "* [3]

Peter's the big brother in the band of disciples. He's the one Jesus calls "Rock", a man of boulder size conviction and avalanche-like action. Once he begins to roll down a hill, he doesn't stop until he hits the bottom. That's why he's in the Garden next to Jesus. He's the one who promised that, though all others would desert Jesus, he would never fall away. He's the one who pledged to be with his Brother to the end, even if it meant death. He spoke those words out of conviction and now—passionately convicted—he's standing by them.

As the detachment of soldiers approaches, Peter draws a sword. He lunges forward and the avalanche begins. He swirls. He tumbles. He falls. And on the way down, he strikes and severs the right ear of a servant named Malchus. As Peter hits bottom, Jesus grabs his arm and says,

> *"Put away the sword! Shall I not drink the cup the Father has given me?"* [4]

It's not a question; it's an order:

> *"Stop fighting for me, stop fighting with me, and stop fighting against me. Let go of me and let me go to the cross!"*

As the soldiers bind and take Jesus away, Peter sits shattered in the Garden. He was ready to die with him. He was willing to stand by him. He had promised to be there when all others left and he had the bloodstained sword to prove his fidelity. He had kept his word.

But now, Peter has become a pebble of a man, pulverized by the hammers of sorrow and confusion. His convictions have been crushed. The man who was willing to fight six hundred men with a single sword and who—in his zeal—cut off the ear of Malchus, now turns and, through the sharp blade of denial, slashes the ear of his Brother. Three times Peter is asked if he's one of Jesus' disciples. As Jesus listens, three times Peter cuts off any association with him. From now on, Jesus stands alone.

> Abandoned.
> Denied.
> Betrayed.

[1]John 18:2-3 [2]John 18:4-6 [3]John 18:10-11 [4]John 18:11

Reflection

What does it feel like when a friend hands you over into the grasp of an enemy? What does it feel like when someone washes his or her hands of you?

In what ways have you abandoned, denied, or betrayed Christ?

Has the *Betrayed Christ* ever told you to put your sword away? If so, what were you fighting for and what was he asking you to do?

What comfort is there in knowing that, even as he was betrayed, the *Betrayed Christ* was still in control?

The Sentenced Christ

Scripture Reading: John 18:28–19:16

Prayer

Father,

After the Sanhedrin falsely convicted your Son of blasphemy, they brought him before Pontius Pilate to be sentenced to death. They wanted an execution and they wanted that execution to bear the curse of crucifixion:

> "No stones. We want him to hang limp on a tree and bear the scourge of God."

But when Pilate interrogated Jesus, he found no crime, no basis for a charge, and therefore no cause for the sentence of the cross. He found him to be as meek as a lamb and as gentle as a dove. Jesus was no threat to Rome. Where there was no threat, no punishment was deserved.

But outside Pilate's palace, the Sanhedrin wanted blood. They shouted, "Crucify him!" They demanded his death. And when given the option of freeing Jesus or Barabbas, they chose the mercenary over the Messiah.

During this day, help me understand the spiritual inequity of the cross as well as its necessity. Help me believe that the *Sentenced Christ* accepted the punishment for sin even though he didn't commit the crime. This day, may I draw peace from this decision and forgiveness from its consequence. It's in his name I pray. Amen.

Meditation

The Sanhedrin is the highest Jewish court in Jerusalem. It's composed of the three groups of people that Jesus had said would deliver him unto death: the elders, chief priests, and teachers of the law.

> *"From that time on Jesus began to explain to his disciples that he must go to Jerusalem and suffer many things at the hands of the elders, chief priests and teachers of the law, and that he must be killed and on the third day be raised to life."* [1]

During the early morning hours that followed Jesus' betrayal and arrest in the Garden, the seventy-one members of the Sanhedrin met under the cloak of darkness. In the safety of the shadows, the high priest, Caiaphas, asked only for damning evidence.

There was none. The court produced false witnesses and trumped up claims of blasphemy. But even then, none of the solicited statements agreed. It was only when the high priest asked Jesus, "Are you the Messiah?" and when Jesus answered, "I am" that a verdict was delivered. [2]

At this, the high priest tore his clothes and the entire Sanhedrin condemned him. The death penalty was set, but the death sentence required the approval of the Roman procurator, Pontius Pilate. And so early in the morning, the Jews led Jesus to the palace of the Roman governor.

But as Pilate interrogates Jesus, he finds no crime. He finds no basis for a charge and therefore no cause for the sentence of the cross. Even though this Jesus may claim to be a King—a heavenly King—Pilate doesn't consider this otherworldly kingdom to be any type of threat to his Rome. And where there is no threat to Rome, there is no need for punishment. He announces his verdict,

"I find no basis for a charge against him." [3]

Instead, as is the custom at Passover, Pilate offers to pardon one prisoner slated for execution. He asks the crowd if they want "the King of the Jews" but to his astonishment they shout back,

"No, not him! Give us Barabbas!" [4]

They choose a mercenary over the Messiah.

Inside the palace, Jesus stands like a lamb ready to be led to the slaughter. Outside the palace gates, the wolves of the Sanhedrin are circling, salivating, and beginning to howl. They want blood. They came asking for it and they won't stop until they get a taste of it in their mouths. Pilate tries to appease the crowd. Again he declares his verdict and presents the King of the Jews to his so-called subjects. But again the kingdom revolts.

" 'Here is your king,' Pilate said to the Jews.

> *But they shouted, 'Take him away! Take him away! Crucify him!'*

> *'Shall I crucify your king?' Pilate asked.*

> *'We have no king but Caesar,' the chief priests answered.*

> *Finally, Pilate handed him over to them to be crucified."* [5]

"Crucify him!" It's a death chant.

But the wolves in the crowd want more than his death; they want his damnation. They want his body to hang from a tree. That's the only acceptable death for this blasphemer: cursed, forsaken, and forever separated from God.

"If a man guilty of a capital offense is put to death and his body is hung on a tree, you must not leave his body on the tree overnight. Be sure to bury him that same day, because anyone who is hung on a tree is under God's curse." [6]

Finally, Pilate accedes.
He gives the order: "Crucify him."

The death sentence is pronounced though a crime has never been committed. What's more astonishing is that the *Sentenced Christ* accepts the punishment. He takes the curse of the cross, carries the punishment for sin on his back, and begins his final steps toward Calvary. He goes in love. He goes because he knows that the curse will bring a blessing.

"Christ redeemed us from the curse of the law by becoming a curse for us, for it is written: 'Cursed is everyone who is hung on a tree.' " [7]

---

[1]Matthew 16:21 [2]Matthew 26:57-68 [3]John 18:38 [4]John 18:40 [5]John 19:14-16 [6]Deuteronomy 21:22-23 [7]Galatians 3:13

Reflection

Why did the death sentence of Christ have to be crucifixion?

How did the curse of the cross turn out to be a blessing for you?

In what ways have you stood in the crowd and yelled, "Take him away! Crucify him!"?

Why was it necessary for the *Sentenced Christ* to go to the cross—innocent of any crime?

Day Thirty-Eight:
The Crucified Christ

Scripture Reading: Matthew 27:27-44

Prayer

Father,

After your Son was sentenced, he accepted the curse of the cross. When the hammer of sin's punishment was raised, he opened his hands and received the nails. And though the spikes fastened his flesh to the cross, it was his love that kept him there. When he was stripped, exposed, and humiliated, he didn't cover himself with the righteous robe of his innocence. Rather, he cloaked himself with the shroud of sin and wrapped himself in the rags of the world's iniquities.

When the evil one derided him through the taunts and insults of the crowd, when he challenged him to prove himself to be the Son of God, and tempted him to forsake the suffering and come down from the cross, your Son clung fast to the nails. He chose to stay high and lifted up. He chose to suffer agony, endure mockery, and bear blasphemy. He chose the cross.

During this day let me live in the sober reality of the crucifixion. Help me understand that, though the sacrifice of the *Crucified Christ* was universal, it was also personal. It was for me. My nails. My sins. My punishment. And as I embrace this humbling gift of grace, burn into my heart the truth that the greatest act of sacrifice was not the fact that the *Crucified Christ* was fastened to the cross, but that he chose to stay there—for me. It's in his name I pray. Amen.

Meditation

Rome reserved the cross for only the worst of criminals.

It was a slow, painful, and degrading way to die. When Jesus reached Golgotha, the Place of the Skull, the Governor's soldiers stripped him of his clothes. They threw him to the ground, spread his arms, and nailed each hand to the crossbeam that Simon of Cyrene had carried. Then they hoisted him into the air, lined his body up with an upright, stationary beam, and—when the two beams were fastened in place—they nailed his feet. His body hangs contorted, twisted, and disfigured. He is the man from whom men hid their faces. [1]

In order to open his chest cavity to breathe, Jesus has to push up with his legs while pulling up and out with his arms. With every breath comes a violent and excruciating seizure of pain. And, though his wounds are painful, they aren't fatal. His agony could last for days.

> *"When they had crucified him, they divided up his clothes by casting lots. And sitting down, they kept watch over him there. Above his head they placed the written charge against him: THIS IS JESUS, THE KING OF THE JEWS.*
>
> *Two robbers were crucified with him, one on his right and one on his left. Those who passed by hurled insults at him, shaking their heads and saying, 'You who are going to destroy the temple and build it in three days, save yourself! Come down from the cross, if you are the Son of God!'* " [2]

Crucifixion is a public form of execution but it also serves as a public warning. Right above the head of the crucified, the crime is always posted, as if to say to all who pass by, "Do this crime. Receive this punishment." The sign above Jesus reads,

"THIS IS THE KING OF THE JEWS".

Though the statement is true, the accompanying death sentence is false. The sign says he's innocent but the cross says he's guilty. On the Place of the Skull, the only testimony to Jesus' innocence is the sign. As it stands at the top of the cross, it trumpets to all who pass by, "Hail to the King of the Jews. Hail King Jesus!"

But the crowds don't listen. To add injury to injustice, they insult the King.

> *"In the same way the chief priests, the teachers of the law and the elders mocked him. 'He saved others,' they said, 'but he can't save himself! He's the King of Israel! Let him come down now from the cross, and we will believe in him. He trusts in God. Let God rescue him now if he wants him, for he said, I am the Son of God.'"* [3]

They don't bow their heads or bend their knees; instead, they pick up rocks of ridicule and hurl them at his spirit. They have bloodied his body and now they want to bruise his soul. Blow after blow, they mock, insult, and deride him. What the mockers don't know is that though they reject the King, he still remains a King. Whether he hangs from a cross or sits on a throne, whether he wears a twisted circle of thorns or a crown of gold, whether he clothes himself in the crimson blood of righteousness or a mantle of glory, the Messianic King will still rule. He will reign.

And so, the crux of the crucifixion is not whether or not the King is a king. Instead, it is found in what Jesus chooses to do when faced with death.

As he hangs on the cross, will he choose to save himself, as he saved so many others, or will he choose to save his world? Will it be his death or their death?

He can only choose one.

Justice won't let him have both. A payment is demanded. Either he would have to pay the penalty for sin or his world would. It was either his blood or theirs.

With eternity in mind and all of humanity in his sight, he makes his choice. He clings fast to the nails. He chooses to stay high and lifted up. He chooses to suffer agony, endure mockery, and bear blasphemy. He grips the cross. And when he finally breathes his last, he gasps, lets go of the cross, opens his hands, and gives his parting gift—grace.

> *"Surely he took up our infirmities*
> *and carried our sorrows,*
> *yet we considered him stricken by God,*
> *smitten by him, and afflicted.*
> *But he was pierced for our transgressions,*
> *he was crushed for our iniquities;*
> *the punishment that brought us peace*
> *was upon him,*
> *and by his wounds we are healed.*
> *We all, like sheep, have gone astray,*
> *each of us has turned to his own way;*
> *and the LORD has laid on him the iniquity*
> *of us all."* [4]

[1]Isaiah 53:3 [2]Matthew 27:35-40 [3]Matthew 27: 41-43 [4]Isaiah 53:4-6

Reflection

What kept the *Crucified Christ* hanging on the cross?

Why did Jesus have to endure such a painful death?

In what ways have you stood in the crowd and insulted the *Crucified Christ?*

What does it mean when the prophet Isaiah says that the *Crucified Christ* was, "pierced for our transgressions" and "crushed for our iniquities"?

Day Thirty-Nine:
The Dying Christ

Scripture Reading: Matthew 27:45-56

Prayer

Father,

As your Son was dying, darkness came over the land and smothered the brightest part of the day. For three hours one Friday, the light that came from your Fatherly presence was eclipsed by the curse of a prodigal world's sin. And as that sin passed in front of your holiness, a shadow of separation and a pall of judgment fell on your Son. Though he knew no sin, he became sin for us. And when he became sin, you abandoned him. You turned your face from him even though he was your One and Only Son. Like any child who is afraid of the dark he screamed, "Father, where are you?" Yet you hid your face and closed your ears. You left him alone in the darkness. Forsaken. You abandoned him and let him hang on the cross because, in the saving plan of your heaven, a forsaken Son meant a forgiven world. On this day, Father, you so loved the world that you gave up your only Son.

During this day, create faith in me to believe that the *Dying Christ* died because of, for, and in place of me. Overwhelm me with the realization that he took all of my sins upon himself and—in exchange—gave me all of his righteousness. He died so that I might live. He was forsaken so that I might be forgiven. And in the darkness of my days, comfort me with the truth that he bore abandonment, separation, and the punishment of sin so that I would never have to. It's in his name I pray. Amen.

Meditation

It's the sixth hour and the heavenly Father has just dropped his One and Only Son on the Devil's doorstep. He has given him up, abandoned him, and forsaken him. The Son of God has become an orphan. And when the bell rings at the ninth hour, death will answer the door.

> *"From the sixth hour until the ninth hour darkness came over all the land. About the ninth hour Jesus cried out in a loud voice, 'Eloi, Eloi, lama sabachthani?'—which means, 'My God, my God, why have you forsaken me?' "* [1]

As Jesus hangs on the cross, the sun seems to have fallen from the sky. It's noon and yet it looks like midnight. It's an earthly image of a heavenly reality. Jesus is in his eleventh hour and the Light of the World is about to be extinguished.

Soon, Lucifer, the fallen morning star, will toll the bell of his death. Darkness has covered the land. With the shroud of darkness come the sounds of death: moans, wails, the last whispers of life, and the rattle of death. In his final moments, he screams,

> *"My God, my God, why have you forsaken me?"* [2]

To die on a cross is torture but to die alone is torment.

> *"But your iniquities have separated you from your God; your sins have hidden his face from you, so that he will not hear."* [3]

His cross is made up of two intersecting beams—sin and death. Sin is the cause and death is the consequence. As Jesus grips the nails, he grabs hold of sin. He reaches back into history and forward into eternity and, as he does, he takes upon himself all of the world's sin—past, present, and future. He bears every shameful, deplorable, and immoral act his world had, would, and could ever commit.

But he just doesn't bear sin; he becomes it. And because he embodies it, he must now also embrace the consequence: spiritual separation from his Father and physical death. To bear one of the two is painful, but to bear both is excruciating. Because he has become sin, he must die. Because he is sin, he must die alone.

As he hangs on the cross, his Father rejects his plea but accepts his payment. Though Jesus has been forsaken, his world has been forgiven. Knowing that his work is accomplished, he lifts his head toward heaven and—with one last push of his legs—he opens his lungs and gathers enough breath to cry out in a loud voice,

"It is finished!"

After that, he bows his head, gives up his spirit, and embraces death. And when the Son of Heaven dies, all of earth begins to testify.

"At that moment the curtain of the temple was torn in two from top to bottom. The earth shook and the rocks split. The tombs broke open and the bodies of many holy people who had died were raised to life." 4

Only nature knows what has just happened.

His last breath split the rocks, shook the earth, opened tombs, and raised the dead. The force of the events declares his power, while the result declares his purpose; he has died in order to give life.

Though his body will soon be taken down from the cross, placed in a tomb, and sealed with a stone, on the third day that tomb will open. Then death will be defeated.

His last breath also brings reconciliation.

As his head falls, his hands tear the veil of the Holy of Holies. It's ripped from top to bottom, from heaven to earth, from God to man. Now the Father is accessible. He is approachable.

> No more separation between God and man.
> No more need for a mediator.
> No more sacrifices for sin.
> No more blood on the altar.

The last sacrifice—the Lamb of God—has been slain. Sin's debt has been paid. The High Priest has entered the Most Holy place once for all, and he has invited his people to draw near to the Father.

> *"Therefore, brothers, since we have confidence to enter the Most Holy Place by the blood of Jesus, by a new and living way opened for us through the curtain, that is, his body, and since we have a great priest over the house of God, let us draw near to God with a sincere heart in full assurance of faith, having our hearts sprinkled to cleanse us from a guilty conscience and having our bodies washed with pure water."* [5]

[1]Matthew 27:45-46 [2]Matthew 27:46 [3]Isaiah 59:2 [4]Matthew 27:51-52
[5]Hebrews 10:19-22

Reflection

In what ways have you cried out, "My God, my God why have you forsaken me?"

Why did the Father forsake the *Dying Christ?* Why did darkness, abandonment, and silence characterize Jesus' last hours?

Why did Jesus have to die? How can the death of one man give life to all men?

Why was the temple curtain torn in two? How does that act change your relationship with God?

Day Forty:
The Resurrected Christ

Scripture Reading: John 19:38–20:18

Prayer

Father,

After your Son had died, Joseph of Arimathea and Nicodemus asked Pilate for his body. They took him down from the cross and carried him to a garden tomb. In haste, they anointed his body with spices made of myrrh and aloe and then wrapped it in strips of linen. When they had finished, they sealed the tomb with a stone.

As the stone slammed into place, all of their dreams were locked inside. The grave had swallowed up their hope. Death had taken the last breath out of the Messiah. And so they left the garden believing that this was the end: not just the end of *his* life, but the beginning of the end of *their* lives.

But early in the morning, on the first day of the week, his life began again. Mary Magdalene went to the tomb and found the stone rolled away. She saw the grave clothes but his body was missing. Her first thought was, "Grave robbers! They have rolled the stone away and have taken his body."

But as she wept in the garden, the Resurrected Christ came to her. He called in a soft and tender voice, "Mary." And when she heard her name, she knew that he was alive. He had moved the stone. And on the way out, he robbed the grave of its victory.

Father, like the women who made their way to the tomb on the first day of the week, gloom leads my way. My hope is buried. Fear entombs me. And sorrow shatters my dreams and seals me in. Like Mary Magdalene, tears blur my eyes.

But on this day, I ask that, in the graveyard of my life, the *Resurrected Christ* would speak my name. And when I hear my name, may I turn and see the Ever-Living Jesus. It's his voice I listen for and it's in his name I pray. Amen.

Meditation

When Jesus dies, secret love goes public.

Joseph of Arimethea, a wealthy yet discreet disciple, provided the tomb. Nicodemus, one of the Sanhedrin members who had earlier visited Jesus by night, brought the spices. Fear of the Jews had kept these two high profile men from revealing their hearts earlier. After all, they had much to lose—prestige, position, power. But they also knew that, in Jesus, they had much to gain.

While Jesus was alive, they never took a stand. They never got involved. They kept their faith quiet. But now that he's dead, they're willing to risk it all.

They go to Pilate and ask for his body. They carry it to a garden tomb, anoint it with seventy-five pounds of spices, wrap it with strips of linen, and then seal the tomb with a stone. These men are silent no longer. One has given his tomb; the other has brought his spices. This

Jesus is their Jesus. His death is their death. Little do they know that on the third day, his life will be their life.

> *"Early on the first day of the week, while it was still dark, Mary Magdalene went to the tomb and saw that the stone had been removed from the entrance. So she came running to Simon Peter and the other disciple, the one Jesus loved, and said, 'They have taken the Lord out of the tomb, and we don't know where they have put him!' "* [1]

Mary Magdalene knew what it was like to be entombed. She once had seven demons living within her! They bound her in fear, wrapped her in despair, and sealed her in darkness. She was among the living dead, buried alive. But when Jesus spoke her name, the demons left. She was alive again. Resurrected.

But now the one who freed her from her tomb is missing from his. The stone's been rolled away, the grave clothes are still there, but his body is gone. Immediately, she runs and tells Simon Peter and the "disciple whom Jesus loved",

> *"They have taken the Lord out of the tomb, and we don't know where they have put him!"* [2]

Together, they all run back to the tomb. Simon and the other disciple enter the tomb and notice that the strips of linen are still intact and the burial cloth that had been around his head was folded up by itself. No disorder. No disarray. This isn't the work of thieves. They know that he's not in the tomb but they don't know what to believe beyond that.

Confused, the two disciples go back home. Crushed, Mary stays outside the tomb and weeps. As she weeps, she rocks her body. When she leans forward, she can see inside the tomb. When she leans back, she only sees the stone. As she leans forward into the tomb, she sees two angels in white and they ask her why she's crying.

> " 'They have taken my Lord away,' she said, 'and I don't know where they have put him.' At this, she turned around and saw Jesus standing there, but she did not realize that it was Jesus.
>
> 'Woman,' he said, 'why are you crying? Who is it you are looking for?' Thinking he was the gardener, she said, 'Sir, if you have carried him away, tell me where you have put him, and I will get him.'
>
> Jesus said to her, 'Mary.' " [3]

He speaks her name.

When she hears her name, she recognizes his voice. It's the same voice that called out her name in the darkness of the seven demons. It's the same voice that she followed when she went from town to town, village to village, listening to him proclaim the good news of the kingdom of God. It's the same voice that she heard while she was beneath the cross. And now, once again, this voice speaks her name. When he says, "Mary", her weeping stops, her eyes clear, and she sees his face. The one that she loves is alive.

Alive!

She can't keep the news to herself.

> "Mary Magdalene went to the disciples with the news: 'I have seen the Lord!' And she told them that he had said these things to her." [4]

> She's seen the Lord!
> > He's alive!
> > > He spoke her name!

[1]John 20:1-2 [2]John 20:2 [3]John 20:13-16 [4]John 20:18

Reflection

Do you have any secret love for the *Crucified Christ* that needs to go public?

What graveyards are there in your life?
What stones do you need rolled away?

What tears are blurring your eyes from seeing the *Resurrected Christ?*

In what way has the *Resurrected Christ* spoken your name? Who do you need to tell the good news, "I have seen the Lord!"?

Sabbath Day of Resurrection

"Why do you look for the living among the dead? He is not here; he has risen!"

Luke 24:5

He's alive!

Yet, all too many times, we insist on looking for the *Resurrected Christ* among the dead. We go to the tomb. We look at the burial cloth. We weep in the darkness.

On this Sabbath day, the angels invite us to look beyond death, past the grave, through the tears, and into his resurrected and glorious face. They trumpet the good news,

"He is not here; he has risen!"

Reflection

At what tomb are you sitting, wondering where your Savior is?

The angels declared, "He is not here; he has risen!" How could that one sentence change your life?

How is Christ raising you from the dead?

As You Begin Again

Look back at the prayer that you wrote before you began the journey. How has that prayer been answered?

In what ways have you come "to know Christ" during this journey? How have you shared in his sufferings as well as his resurrection?

What is your next journey?
Where is the next adventure leading?
How will you begin?

As you end this leg of the journey and make preparations to begin another, write a prayer. Thank Christ for what he has done and express your heart's desire for the next journey.

Epilogue

The experts say, "Write what you know!"

In the case of this book, I broke with that piece of advice. For me, writing this book was a new and different spiritual journey. Desire drove me to write it, not knowledge. A prayer was behind every word, thought, and phrase that I chose:

"I want to know Christ!"

As I wrote, I wanted to learn more about him. I wanted to become more and more like him. I wanted to suffer, die, and rise with him. All three have happened.

Upon reflection, the best part of the journey has been realizing anew—as if for the first time—that the Christ whom I had hoped to know already knew me. Before I thought to pray the prayer above—and long before I began this book—he knew me.

He knows my dreams, my deepest desires, my sin, and my shame. He knows my future and he knows my past. But he just doesn't know about me. He knows me. He cares more about my relationship with him than I do. He wants to draw me close to himself and he knows how to do it. Tenderly. Gently. He woos and welcomes.

When this epiphany came, it was a "summit moment." Rare spiritual air. Clear vision. A beautiful vista. Like Peter on the Mount of Transfiguration, I found myself saying,

"Lord, it is good for me to be here."

Hopefully, throughout the book, you have had a similar experience. Better yet, I hope you found yourself saying,

"Lord, it is good for *you* to be here."

On the "summit," I realized, in a new way, that Jesus the Christ is always present. Incarnate. Word made flesh. Always dwelling among us. He is in any and every season of my life. From eternity, he has journeyed toward me.

It was my prayer that, as you read this book, you would experience his presence and—through that—you would come to know him. Admittedly, the fulfillment of that prayer is a process and it comes through a journey. I've found that journey to be ...

> Personal,
>> Passionate,
>>> and Intimate.

During the time that it took to write this book, Jesus the Christ went out of his way to encounter me. As he did with the woman at the well, he met me where I was. He accepted me as I was. But he didn't leave me that way. Instead, he began to transform me. After the journey, the relationship was no longer the same. He hadn't changed. I had.

Postscript

When I started this journey I prayed, "I want to know Christ." I began hoping to encounter Christ. Mistakenly, I was under the illusion that—as the journey progressed—Christ and I would meet somewhere in the middle. He would approach from the back and I would come from the front, like two hikers meeting and then passing on a trail. Little did I realize that, before I took my first step, he had walked up alongside me. He was there from the start.

We had walked this path together.

I've reached my destination, finished what I started, and accomplished what I set out to do—forty days complete! I do know Christ! Not absolutely. Not fully. But I do know him more intimately.

The unexpected prize is that I came to know—in a deeply moving and astounding way—that, before I ever set out to know him, he set out to know me.

paul

January 13, 2003

If this book has helped you know Christ,
we'd like to hear from you.

Faith Lutheran Church
37635 Dequindre Road • Troy, Michigan 48083 USA
(248) 689-4664 • www.faithtroy.org • contact@faithtroy.org